WITH ONE VOICE

A Lutheran Resource for Worship

Augsburg Fortress
Minneapolis

WITH ONE VOICE
A Lutheran Resource for Worship

Pew Edition

Also available:
Accompaniment Edition (3-302)
Leaders Edition (3-303)
Instrumental Parts (3-304)
Cassette Recording of the Liturgies (3-305)

The paper used in this publication meets the minimum requirements of American National Standards for Information Sciences—Permanence of Paper for Printed Library Materials, ANSI Z329.48-1984.

Manufactured in the U.S.A.   ISBN 0-8066-0051-9   AF 3-301

03 02 01 00 99 98 97 96 95   4 5 6 7 8 9 10 11 12 13 14 15

CONTENTS

INTRODUCTION

With One Voice has been prepared as an additional volume of resources for Lutherans at worship. It is intended to stand beside the principal worship book presently in use and to supplement its contents.

Several premises underlie the preparation of this collection. *With One Voice* is oriented primarily to the principal weekly assembly of God's people. These new liturgical settings, hymns, and songs are offered to assist those who gather around the Word and Sacraments, and to support the lectionary as it unfolds the saving story through the seasons of the Christian year.

The title suggests another focus of the volume. The letter to the Romans contains the exhortation to "live in harmony with one another…that together you may with one voice glorify…God" (Romans 15:5–6). A quick glance at this resource will reveal that to sing "with one voice" does not imply uniformity of expression. The "one voice" of the Church represents an amazingly diverse fabric, many songs of many cultures in many styles, woven together by the one Spirit. The size of *With One Voice* allows only a sampling of these many songs, but the breadth represented here is a witness to the Church's unity in diversity and an encouragement to communities to cultivate a variety of expressions when they gather, rather than dividing themselves by style of worship or music.

The liturgy of Holy Communion in *With One Voice* continues to "embody the tradition of worship which received its characteristic shape during the early centuries of the Church's existence and was reaffirmed during the Reformation era" (Introduction, *Lutheran Book of Worship*). The design of the services in this volume aims to reveal this characteristic shape. Two services of Holy Communion (*Light of Christ* and *Bread of Life*) are presented with complete musical settings. Holy Communion: *All Times and Places,* Setting 6, follows the model of Martin Luther's Chorale Service and suggests the insertion of service music from a wide variety of sources to be used for the principal musical elements. It is a flexible structure enabling the celebration of Holy Communion with integrity while allowing for adaptation to various circumstances.

This resource includes also a Service of Word and Prayer, incorporating service music, proclamation of the Word, creed and confession, offering and prayer.

The many songs gathered together in the hymn collection of *With One Voice* include a large number that have already found their way into the repertoire of many Lutheran assemblies. In addition to well-loved hymns from several traditions, there are contributions from the diverse cultures of North America as well as a representative sampling of materials from other parts of the world. Songs that center around a repeated refrain (choruses, materials from Taizé) stand alongside the lively poetry and new melodies of the "hymnic explosion" of the last two decades. Strong and singable melodies have been prized in every genre represented. Accompaniments are included throughout for the hymns and songs in order to enable the use of these materials in a variety of settings and to enable singing in harmony where appropriate.

Throughout this supplementary resource careful attention has been given to the use of language that includes all God's people and employs a broadened palette of images for the persons of the Trinity. Liturgical texts are in continuity with those prepared for *LBW*, incorporating several further revisions of the English Language Liturgical Consultation (an ecumenical group representing major English-speaking churches) published in *Praying Together* (1988). The ELLC versions of the Apostles' and Nicene Creeds are provided on pages 54–55, and congregations are encouraged to study them for possible use.

Thirty years ago, Lutherans in North America entered into a significant process in the development of common worship resources as the Inter-Lutheran Commission on Worship undertook work leading toward a renewal in the worship life of the Lutheran churches. In the intervening years, the rapid change of contemporary society has confronted the world and the Church. While the fundamental pattern of the Church's worship does not change, the ways that Christians at worship express themselves in word, music, and gesture are always unfolding. Developed by the Publishing House and the Division for Congregational Ministries of the Evangelical Lutheran Church in America, with consultation and review provided by congregations and lay persons, church musicians and pastors, theologians and ecumenical partners, *With One Voice* is offered as a further vehicle for the richly varied and constantly emerging praise and prayer of the Church.

May *With One Voice* be a useful instrument so that "joined together in harmony and having received the godly melody in unison, you might sing in one voice through Jesus Christ…that you might always partake of God."

(*Ephesians IV*, Ignatius of Antioch, c. 35–c. 107 A.D.)

> It is the voice of the Church that is heard in singing together.
> It is not you that sings, it is the Church that is singing,
> and you, as a member of the Church, may share in its song.
> Thus all singing together…serves to widen our spiritual horizon,
> make us see our little company as a member
> of the great Christian Church on earth,
> and help us willingly and gladly to join our singing,
> be it feeble or good,
> to the song of the Church.
>
> Dietrich Bonhöffer, *Life Together*

In addition to the Pew Edition, an Accompaniment Edition with complete liturgical music and the entire collection of hymns and songs with additional alternate harmonizations is available, as well as a Leaders Edition, which supplies materials needed by those who plan and conduct worship. All three editions are necessary in order for *With One Voice* to be used to its full potential.

FOUNDATIONS FOR THE CHRISTIAN ASSEMBLY

From the earliest days of the Church, Christian worship has been marked by a pattern of gathering, word, meal, and sending. These basic elements—revealed in the New Testament, the writings of the early Church, the Lutheran confessions, and ecumenical documents—constitute the center of the Church's worship.

Beginning with Moses and all the prophets, Jesus interpreted to them the things about himself in all the scriptures. ... When he was at table with them, he took bread, blessed and broke it, and gave it to them. Then their eyes were opened and they recognized him.   *Luke 24:27, 30–31a*

The baptized devoted themselves to the apostles' teaching and fellowship, to the breaking of bread and the prayers.   *Acts 2:42*

On Sunday all are gathered together in unity. The records of the apostles or the writings of the prophets are read for as long as time allows. The presider exhorts and invites us into the pattern of these good things. Then we all stand and offer prayer.

When we have concluded the prayer, bread is set out together with wine. ... The presider then offers prayer and thanksgiving and the people sing out their assent, saying the "Amen." There is a distribution of the things over which thanks has been said and each person participates, and these things are sent to those who are not present.

Those who are prosperous give what they wish according to each one's own choice, and the collection is deposited with the presider, who aids orphans and widows, those in want because of disease, those in prison, and foreigners who are staying here.

We hold this meeting together on Sunday since it is the first day, on which God, having transformed darkness and matter, created the world. On the same day Jesus Christ our Savior rose from the dead. On Sunday he appeared to his apostles and disciples and taught them these things which we present to you.

From the Apology of Justin Martyr (c. 150 A.D.)

It is taught among us that one holy Christian church will be and remain forever. This is the assembly of all believers among whom the Gospel is preached in its purity and the holy sacraments are administered according to the Gospel.

For it is sufficient for the true unity of the Christian church that the Gospel be preached in conformity with a pure understanding of it and that the sacraments be administered in accordance with the divine Word. It is not necessary for the true unity of the Christian church that humanly instituted ceremonies should be observed uniformly in all places.

Augsburg Confession VII (1530)

The Church earnestly desires that all the faithful be led to that full, conscious, and active participation in liturgical celebrations called for by the very nature of the liturgy. Such participation by the Christian people as "a chosen race, a royal priesthood, a holy nation, God's own people" (1 Peter 2:9; see 2:4–5) is their right and duty by reason of their baptism.

Constitution on the Liturgy, Second Vatican Council (1963)

The services of *Lutheran Book of Worship* embody the tradition of worship which received its characteristic shape during the early centuries of the Church's existence and was reaffirmed during the Reformation era. ...

Freedom and flexibility in worship is a Lutheran inheritance, and there is room for ample variety in ceremony, music, and liturgical form. Having considered their resources and their customs, congregations will find their own balance between fully using the ritual and musical possibilities of the liturgy, and a more modest practice. A full service should not allow secondary ceremonies to eclipse central elements of the liturgy, nor should a simple service omit essential or important parts.

Every service, whether elaborate or spare, sung or said, should be within the framework of the common rite of the Church, so that the integrity of the rite is always respected and maintained.

Lutheran Book of Worship (1978)

HOLY COMMUNION
Shape of the Rite

Sunday is the primary day on which the Church assembles: the first day of creation when God transformed darkness into light and the day on which Christ rose from death and revealed himself to the disciples in the scriptures and the breaking of the bread. The baptized gather to hear the word, to pray for those in need, to offer thanks to God for the gift of salvation, to receive the bread of life and the cup of blessing, and to be renewed for the daily witness of faith, hope, and love. To guests, strangers, and all in need, the Church offers these good things of God's grace.

GATHERING

Entrance Hymn
GREETING
Kyrie
Hymn of Praise
PRAYER OF THE DAY

God calls and gathers believers through the Holy Spirit, and in response the community acclaims this gracious God in song and prayer. The gathering of the congregation may begin with a confession of sin and/or an entrance hymn. God's welcome is extended to the congregation by the presider. When appropriate, a litany or hymn of praise may be sung immediately before the prayer of the day. Through these actions, the congregation prepares to hear the Word of God.

WORD

FIRST READING
Psalm
Second Reading
Gospel Acclamation
GOSPEL
SERMON
HYMN OF THE DAY
Creed
THE PRAYERS

In the rich treasure of Scripture proclaimed by readers and preachers, the Church hears the good news of God acting in this and every time and place. A three-year cycle of readings provides portions of the Hebrew Scriptures, the New Testament letters, and the Gospel books for each week. During Advent/Christmas, the lectionary reveals the mystery of the Word made flesh. In Lent/Easter, the paschal mystery of the Lord's death and resurrection is proclaimed. Throughout the Season after Pentecost, the New Testament texts are read in a continuous order. During the last Sundays of the year, the readings present the final vision of a new heaven and a new earth.

This encounter with the living Word, Jesus Christ, is marked by proclamation and silence, psalm and hymn, singing and speaking, movement and gesture. Silence after the readings allows time for the word to be pondered. The sermon announces good news for the community and the world; the hymn of the day both proclaims and responds to the word; a creed is a further response to it. God's Word, read and preached and acclaimed, leads the community to pray for the Church, the people of the world, and those who suffer or are in need.

MEAL

Greeting of Peace
PRESENTATION OF THE GIFTS
GREAT THANKSGIVING
LORD'S PRAYER
COMMUNION
Canticle
Prayer

In thanksgiving, the congregation praises God for the gracious gifts of creation and the saving deeds of Jesus Christ. To the table of the Lord are brought bread and wine, simple signs of God's love, humble signs of human labor. In word and gesture, prayer and song, the people lift up their hearts in praise and thanksgiving for the gifts of forgiveness, life, and salvation, hearing Jesus' words spoken at this supper, remembering his death and resurrection. The presider asks that the Holy Spirit unite the community in the Lord's bread and cup so that, as one body in Christ, it too might proclaim God's salvation in the world. To this grateful proclamation, the community joins its "Amen" before praying the Lord's Prayer with one voice. Welcomed to the table, each one is united with God in Christ, with each other, and with the Church's mission in the world. During the communion, hymns, songs, and psalms may be sung. As the table is cleared, the congregation may sing a canticle. A brief prayer concludes the liturgy of the meal.

SENDING

BLESSING
Dismissal

Worship on the Lord's Day ends with simplicity. The community receives the blessing of God. All are invited to leave in peace, sent out to serve in word and deed: to speak the words of good news they have heard, to care for those in need, and to share what they have received with the poor and the hungry.

Central elements of the Holy Communion liturgy are noted in uppercase letters; other elements support and reveal the essential shape of Christian worship.

BRIEF ORDER FOR
CONFESSION AND FORGIVENESS

Stand

The minister leads the congregation in the invocation. The sign of the cross may be made by all in remembrance of their Baptism.

P In the name of the Father, and of the ✝ Son, and of the Holy Spirit.
C **Amen**

The minister continues, using one of the sections below.

OR

P Almighty God,
to whom all hearts are open,
all desires known,
and from whom no secrets are hid:
Cleanse the thoughts of our hearts
by the inspiration of your Holy Spirit,
that we may perfectly love you
and worthily magnify your holy name,
through Jesus Christ our Lord. (236)
C **Amen**

P God of all mercy and consolation,
come to the aid of your people,
turning us from our sin
to live for you alone.
Give us the power of your Holy Spirit
that, attentive to your Word,
we may confess our sins,
receive your forgiveness,
and grow into the fullness of your Son,
Jesus Christ our Lord. (574)
C **Amen**

P If we say we have no sin,
we deceive ourselves,
and the truth is not in us.
But if we confess our sins,
God who is faithful and just
will forgive our sins
and cleanse us from all unrighteousness.

P Let us confess our sin in the
presence of God and of one another.

Kneel/Stand

Silence for reflection and self-examination.

P Most merciful God,
C **we confess**
that we are in bondage to sin
and cannot free ourselves.
We have sinned against you
in thought, word, and deed,
by what we have done
and by what we have left undone.
We have not loved you
with our whole heart;
we have not loved
our neighbors as ourselves.
For the sake of your Son, Jesus Christ,
have mercy on us.
Forgive us, renew us, and lead us,
so that we may delight in your will
and walk in your ways,
to the glory of your holy name. Amen

P Gracious God,
C **have mercy on us.**
In your compassion
forgive us our sins,
known and unknown,
things done and left undone.
Uphold us by your Spirit
so that we may live and serve you
in newness of life,
to the honor and glory of your holy name;
through Jesus Christ our Lord. Amen

The minister stands and addresses the congregation.

P In the mercy of almighty God,
Jesus Christ was given to die for us,
and for his sake
God forgives us all our sins.
As a called and ordained minister of the
Church of Christ, and by his authority,
I therefore declare to you
the entire forgiveness of all your sins,
in the name of the Father,
and of the ✢ Son, and of the Holy Spirit.
C **Amen**

P Almighty God have mercy on you,
forgive you all your sins
through our Lord Jesus Christ,
strengthen you in all goodness,
and by the power of the Holy Spirit
keep you in eternal life.
C **Amen**

HOLY COMMUNION
Light of Christ, Setting 4

The Brief Order for Confession and Forgiveness (p. 10) may be used before this service.
The minister may announce the day and its significance before the Entrance Hymn or before
the readings.

GATHERING

Stand

ENTRANCE HYMN or Psalm

GREETING

The minister greets the congregation.

🅿 The grace of our Lord Jesus Christ, the love of God,
and the communion of the Holy Spirit be with you all.
🅒 **And also with you.**

KYRIE

The Kyrie may follow.

🅐 In peace, in peace let us pray to the Lord.   🅐 For the

🅒 Lord, have mer - cy.

peace from a - bove,   and for our sal - va - tion, let us pray to the

Lord.

A For the peace of the whole world, the well-being of the

C Lord, have mer - cy.

Church of God, and for the u-ni-ty of all, let us pray to the

Lord.

A For this ho-ly house, and for all who of-fer here their

C Lord, have mer - cy.

wor-ship and praise, let us pray to the Lord.

C Lord, have mer - cy.

A Help, save, com-fort, and de-fend us, gra-cious Lord.

C A - men

HYMN OF PRAISE

The Hymn of Praise or another appropriate hymn may be sung.

Glo-ry to God in the high - est, and peace to God's peo-ple on earth.

1 Lord God, heav-en-ly king, al-might-y God and Fa-ther, we wor-ship you, we give you thanks, we praise you for your glo - ry.

2 Lord Je - sus Christ, on - ly Son of the Fa - ther, Lord God, Lamb of God, you take a - way the sin of the world: have mer - cy, have mer-cy on us; you are seat - ed at the right hand of the Fa - ther: re - ceive our prayer.

3 For you a - lone are the Ho - ly One, you a - lone are the Lord, you a - lone are the Most High, Je - sus Christ, with the Ho - ly Spir-it, in the glo - ry of God the Fa - ther. A - men.

The Prayer of the Day follows on page 16.

OR

C This is the feast of vic - to - ry for our God.

Al - le - lu - ia, al - le - lu - ia.

I Wor - thy is Christ, the Lamb who was slain, whose

blood set us free to be peo - ple of God.

II Pow - er and rich - es, wis - dom and strength, and

hon - or and bless - ing and glo - ry are his.

C This is the feast of vic - to - ry for our God.

Al - le - lu - ia, al - le - lu - ia.

I Sing with all the peo - ple of God, and

join in the hymn of all cre - a - tion:

>

Ⅲ Bless - ing and hon - or, glo - ry and might to God and the Lamb for - ev - er. A - men

C This is the feast of vic - to - ry for our God. Al - le - lu - ia, al - le - lu - ia.

Ⅰ Ⅲ For the Lamb, the Lamb who was slain has be - gun his reign. Al - le - lu - ia.

C This is the feast of vic - to - ry for our God. Al - le - lu - ia, al - le - lu - ia, al - le - lu - ia. A - men

PRAYER OF THE DAY

The salutation may precede the prayer.

P The Lord be with you.
C And also with you.

P Let us pray. *(The Prayer of the Day is said, concluding:)*
C Amen

WORD

Sit

FIRST READING

A A reading from _____.

After the reading, the reader may say: The word of the Lord.
All may respond: **Thanks be to God.**

PSALM

The Psalm is sung or said.

SECOND READING

A A reading from _____.

After the reading, the reader may say: The word of the Lord.
All may respond: **Thanks be to God.**

Stand

GOSPEL ACCLAMATION

The appointed Verse may be sung by the choir, or the congregation may sing a general acclamation or a hymn.

GENERAL

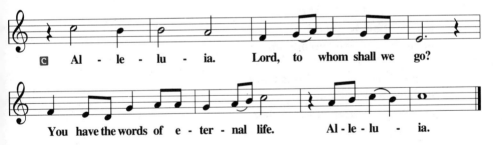

C Al - le - lu - ia. Lord, to whom shall we go?
You have the words of e - ter - nal life. Al - le - lu - ia.

LENT

C Re - turn to the Lord, your God, who is gra - cious and mer - ci - ful,
slow to an - ger, and a - bound - ing in stead - fast love.

GOSPEL

The Gospel is announced.

Ⓟ The Holy Gospel according to _____, the _____ chapter.
Ⓒ **Glory to you, O Lord.**

After the reading:

Ⓟ The Gospel of the Lord.
Ⓒ **Praise to you, O Christ.**

Sit

SERMON

Silence for reflection may follow.

Stand

HYMN OF THE DAY

CREED

A Creed may be said: the Nicene Creed, on all festivals and on Sundays in the seasons of Advent/Christmas and Lent/Easter; the Apostles' Creed, at other times. When Holy Baptism or another rite with a creed is celebrated, this creed may be omitted.

NICENE CREED

Ⓒ **We believe in one God,**
   the Father, the Almighty,
   maker of heaven and earth,
   of all that is, seen and unseen.

We believe in one Lord, Jesus Christ,
   the only Son of God,
   eternally begotten of the Father,
   God from God, Light from Light,
   true God from true God,
   begotten, not made,
   of one Being with the Father.
   Through him all things were made.
   For us and for our salvation
      he came down from heaven;
      by the power of the Holy Spirit
         he became incarnate from the virgin Mary, and was made man.

For our sake he was crucified under Pontius Pilate;
    he suffered death and was buried.
    On the third day he rose again
        in accordance with the Scriptures;
    he ascended into heaven
        and is seated at the right hand of the Father.
He will come again in glory to judge the living and the dead,
    and his kingdom will have no end.

We believe in the Holy Spirit, the Lord, the giver of life,
    who proceeds from the Father and the Son.
    With the Father and the Son he is worshiped and glorified.
    He has spoken through the prophets.
    We believe in one holy catholic and apostolic Church.
    We acknowledge one Baptism for the forgiveness of sins.
    We look for the resurrection of the dead,
        and the life of the world to come. Amen

APOSTLES' CREED

🇨 I believe in God, the Father almighty,
    creator of heaven and earth.

I believe in Jesus Christ, his only Son, our Lord.
    He was conceived by the power of the Holy Spirit
        and born of the virgin Mary.
    He suffered under Pontius Pilate,
        was crucified, died, and was buried.
    He descended into hell.[*]
    On the third day he rose again.
    He ascended into heaven,
        and is seated at the right hand of the Father.
    He will come again to judge the living and the dead.

I believe in the Holy Spirit,
    the holy catholic Church,
    the communion of saints,
    the forgiveness of sins,
    the resurrection of the body,
    and the life everlasting. Amen

*Or, He descended to the dead.

Stand/Kneel

THE PRAYERS

The Prayers begin with these or similar words:

Ⓐ Let us pray for the whole people of God in Christ Jesus, and for all people according to their needs.

Prayers are included for the whole Church, the nations, those in need, the parish, and special concerns. The congregation may be invited to offer other petitions. The minister gives thanks for the faithful departed, especially for those who recently have died.

Each portion of the prayers concludes with these or similar words:

OR

Ⓐ Lord, in your mercy,	Ⓐ Hear us, O God;
Ⓒ hear our prayer.	**Ⓒ your mercy is great.**

The prayers conclude with these or similar words:

Ⓟ Into your hands, O Lord, we commend all for whom we pray, trusting in your mercy; through your Son, Jesus Christ our Lord.
Ⓒ Amen

MEAL

Stand

PEACE

The Peace is shared.

Ⓟ The peace of the Lord be with you always.
Ⓒ And also with you.

The ministers and congregation may greet one another with a gesture of peace, using these or similar words: **Peace be with you.**

Sit

PRESENTATION OF THE GIFTS

The Offering is received as the Lord's Table is prepared.

The appointed Offertory may be sung by the choir as the gifts are presented, or the congregation may sing the following offertory, or an appropriate hymn or psalm may be sung.

Stand

Let the vine-yards be fruit-ful, Lord, fill to the brim our cup of bless-ing. Gath-er a har-vest from the seeds that were sown, that we may be fed, we may be fed with the bread of life. Gath-er the hopes and the dreams of all; u-nite them with the prayers we of-fer now. Grace our ta-ble with your pres-ence, and give us a fore-taste of the feast to come.

After the gifts have been presented, one of these prayers or another offertory prayer is said.

OR

Ⓐ Let us pray.

Ⓐ Blessed are you,
Ⓒ **O Lord our God,**
maker of all things.
Through your goodness
you have blessed us with these gifts.
With them we offer ourselves
to your service
and dedicate our lives
to the care and redemption
of all that you have made,
for the sake of him
who gave himself for us,
Jesus Christ our Lord. Amen (240)

Ⓐ Let us pray.

Ⓐ Merciful God,
Ⓒ **we offer with joy and thanksgiving**
what you have first given us—
our selves,
our time,
and our possessions,
signs of your gracious love.
Receive them
for the sake of him
who offered himself for us,
Jesus Christ our Lord. Amen (239)

GREAT THANKSGIVING

The Great Thanksgiving is begun by the presiding minister.

P The Lord be with you.

P Lift up your hearts.

C And al-so with you.

C We lift them to the Lord.

P Let us give thanks to the Lord our God.

C It is right to give our thanks and praise.

P It is indeed right and salutary that we should at all times and in all places offer thanks... *(Here the minister continues with the proper preface, concluding:)* we praise your name and join their unending hymn:

C Ho - ly, ho - ly, ho - ly Lord,

Lord God of pow'r and might, heav-en and earth are

full of your glo - ry. Ho - san - na in the high - est.

Bless - ed, bless - ed is he who comes in the name of the

Lord. Ho - san - na in the high - est.

The minister continues, using one of the prayers below.

℗ You are indeed holy, O God,
the fountain of all holiness;
you bring light from darkness,
life from death,
speech from silence.

We worship you for our lives
and for the world you give us.
We thank you
for the new world to come
and for the love
that will rule all in all.
We praise you for the grace
shown to Israel, your chosen,
the people of your promise:
the rescue from Egypt,
the gift of the promised land,
the memory of the ancestors,
the homecoming from exile,
and the prophets' words
that will not be in vain.

In all this we bless you
for your only-begotten Son,
who fulfilled and will fulfill
all your promises.

In the night in which he was betrayed,
our Lord Jesus took bread,
and gave thanks; broke it,
and gave it to his disciples,
saying: Take and eat;
this is my body, given for you.
Do this for the remembrance of me.

Again, after supper,
he took the cup, gave thanks,
and gave it for all to drink,
saying: This cup is
the new covenant in my blood,
shed for you and for all people
for the forgiveness of sin.
Do this for the remembrance of me.

This prayer continues on page 24.

OR

℗ Holy, mighty, and merciful Lord,
heaven and earth are full of your glory.

In great love you sent to us Jesus,
your Son, who reached out
to heal the sick and suffering,
who preached good news to the poor,
and who, on the cross,
opened his arms to all.

In the night in which he was betrayed,
our Lord Jesus took bread,
and gave thanks; broke it,
and gave it to his disciples,
saying: Take and eat;
this is my body, given for you.
Do this for the remembrance of me.

Again, after supper,
he took the cup, gave thanks,
and gave it for all to drink,
saying: This cup is
the new covenant in my blood,
shed for you and for all people
for the forgiveness of sin.
Do this for the remembrance of me.

Remembering, therefore,
his death, resurrection, and ascension,
we await his coming in glory.

Pour out your Holy Spirit,
that by this Holy Communion
we may know the unity
we share with all your people
in the body of your Son,
Jesus Christ our Lord.

Through him, with him, in him,
in the unity of the Holy Spirit,
all glory and honor is yours,
almighty Father, now and forever.
ⓒ **Amen**

The Lord's Prayer follows on page 25.

℗ For as often as we eat of this bread and drink from this cup,
we proclaim the Lord's death until he comes.

℗ Therefore, O God, with this bread and cup
we remember the incarnation of your Son:
his human birth and the covenant he made with us.
We remember the sacrifice of his life:
his eating with outcasts and sinners,
and his acceptance of death.
But chiefly we remember his rising from the tomb,
his ascension to the seat of power,
and his sending of the holy and life-giving Spirit.
We cry out for the resurrection of our lives,
when Christ will come again in beauty and power
to share with us the great and promised feast.

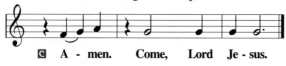

℗ Send now, we pray, your Holy Spirit,
that we and all who share in this bread and cup
may be united in the communion of the Holy Spirit,
may enter the fullness of the kingdom of heaven,
and may receive our inheritance with all your saints in light.

℗ Join our prayers with those of your servants
of every time and every place, and unite them
with the ceaseless petitions of our great high priest
until he comes as victorious Lord of all.
Through him, with him, in him, in the unity of the Holy Spirit,
all glory and honor is yours, almighty Father, now and forever.

LORD'S PRAYER

Ⓟ Let us pray with confidence in the words our Savior gave us:

Ⓒ **Our Father in heaven,
hallowed be your name,
your kingdom come,
your will be done,
on earth as in heaven.
Give us today our daily bread.
Forgive us our sins
as we forgive those
who sin against us.
Save us from the time of trial
and deliver us from evil.
For the kingdom, the power,
and the glory are yours,
now and for ever. Amen**

Ⓟ Lord, remember us in your kingdom, and teach us to pray:

Ⓒ **Our Father, who art in heaven,
hallowed be thy name,
thy kingdom come,
thy will be done,
on earth as it is in heaven.
Give us this day our daily bread;
and forgive us our trespasses,
as we forgive those
who trespass against us;
and lead us not into temptation,
but deliver us from evil.
For thine is the kingdom,
and the power, and the glory,
forever and ever. Amen**

Sit

COMMUNION

The communion follows. The bread may be broken for distribution.
As the ministers give the bread and cup to each communicant, they say these words:
The body of Christ, given for you. The blood of Christ, shed for you.
The communicant may say: **Amen**
As the people commune, hymns and other music may be used, and may include the following:

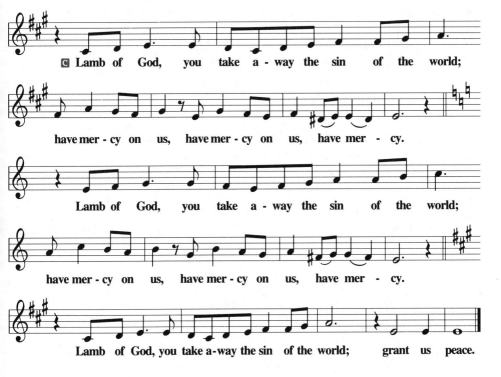

Ⓒ Lamb of God, you take a-way the sin of the world; have mer-cy on us, have mer-cy on us, have mer-cy.

Lamb of God, you take a-way the sin of the world; have mer-cy on us, have mer-cy on us, have mer-cy.

Lamb of God, you take a-way the sin of the world; grant us peace.

Stand

After all have returned to their places, the minister may say these or similar words.

P The body and blood of our Lord Jesus Christ strengthen you
and keep you in his grace.

C **Amen**

CANTICLE

A post-communion canticle or an appropriate hymn or song may be sung.

C Now, Lord, you let your ser - vant go in peace:
your word has been ful - filled. My own eyes have
seen the sal - va - tion which you have pre - pared in the sight of all
peo - ple: a light to re - veal you to the
na - tions and the glo - ry of your peo - ple Is - ra - el.
Glo - ry to the Fa - ther and to the Son, glo - ry to the
Ho - ly Spir - it, as it was in the be - gin - ning, is now, and
will be for - ev - er. A - men, a - men, a - men.

OR

Thank-ful hearts and voic - es raise; tell ev - 'ry - one what God has done. Let all who seek the Lord re - joice, re - joice and bear Christ's ho - ly name. Send us, O God, with your prom - is - es, and lead us forth in joy with shouts of thanks - giv - ing. Al - le - lu - ia, al - le - lu - ia.

PRAYER

The following or a similar post-communion prayer is said.

Ⓐ Let us pray.

Ⓐ Pour out upon us the spirit of your love, O Lord, and unite the wills of those whom you have fed with one heavenly food; through Jesus Christ our Lord. (242)

Ⓒ **Amen**

Silence for reflection.

SENDING

BLESSING

The minister blesses the congregation, using this or another appropriate blessing.

Ⓟ Almighty God, Father, ✛ Son, and Holy Spirit, bless you now and forever.

Ⓒ **Amen**

When there is a procession from the church, a hymn, song, or canticle may be sung.

DISMISSAL

The minister may dismiss the congregation.

Ⓐ Go in peace. Serve the Lord.

Ⓒ **Thanks be to God.**

HOLY COMMUNION
Bread of Life, Setting 5

*The Brief Order for Confession and Forgiveness (p. 10) may be used before this service.
The minister may announce the day and its significance before the Entrance Hymn or before
the readings.*

GATHERING

Stand

ENTRANCE HYMN or Psalm

GREETING

The minister greets the congregation.

℗ The grace of our Lord Jesus Christ, the love of God,
and the communion of the Holy Spirit be with you all.

☙ **And also with you.**

KYRIE

The Kyrie may follow.

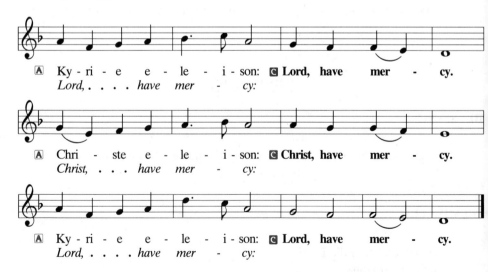

Ⓐ Ky - ri - e   e - le - i - son: ☙ **Lord, have   mer - cy.**
Lord, ... have   mer - cy:

Ⓐ Chri - ste   e - le - i - son: ☙ **Christ, have   mer - cy.**
Christ, . . . have   mer - cy:

Ⓐ Ky - ri - e   e - le - i - son: ☙ **Lord, have   mer - cy.**
Lord, ... have   mer - cy:

HYMN OF PRAISE

The Hymn of Praise or another appropriate hymn may be sung.

© Glo-ry to God, glo-ry to God, glo-ry to God in the high-est;

glo-ry to God, glo-ry to God, and peace to God's peo-ple on earth.

I Lord God, heav-en-ly king, al-might-y God and Fa-ther, we

wor-ship you, we give you thanks, we praise you for your glo-ry.

© Glo-ry to God, glo-ry to God, glo-ry to God in the high-est;

glo-ry to God, glo-ry to God, and peace to God's peo-ple on earth.

II Lord Je-sus Christ, on-ly Son of the Fa-ther,

Lord God, Lamb of God, you take a-way the sin of the

world: have mer-cy on us; you are seat-ed at the

right hand of the Fa-ther: re-ceive our prayer.

C Glo-ry to God, glo-ry to God, glo-ry to God in the high-est;

glo-ry to God, glo-ry to God, and peace to God's peo-ple on earth.

I / II For you a-lone are the Ho-ly One, you a-lone are the Lord,

you a-lone are the Most High, Je-sus Christ, with the Ho-ly Spir-it,

in the glo-ry of God the Fa-ther. A-men.

C Glo-ry to God, glo-ry to God, glo-ry to God in the high-est;

glo-ry to God, glo-ry to God, and peace to God's peo-ple on earth,

and peace to God's peo-ple on earth.

PRAYER OF THE DAY

The salutation may precede the prayer.

P The Lord be with you.

C **And also with you.**

P Let us pray. *(The Prayer of the Day is said, concluding:)*

C **Amen**

WORD

Sit

FIRST READING

Ⓐ A reading from _____.

After the reading, the reader may say: The word of the Lord.
All may respond: **Thanks be to God.**

PSALM

The Psalm is sung or said.

SECOND READING

Ⓐ A reading from _____.

After the reading, the reader may say: The word of the Lord.
All may respond: **Thanks be to God**.

Stand

GOSPEL ACCLAMATION

The appointed verse may be sung by the choir, or the congregation may sing a general acclamation or a hymn.

GENERAL

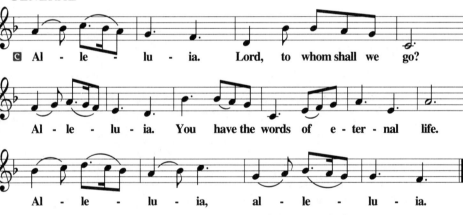

Ⓒ Al - le - lu - ia. Lord, to whom shall we go?
Al - le - lu - ia. You have the words of e - ter - nal life.
Al - le - lu - ia, al - le - lu - ia.

LENT

Ⓒ Re - turn to the Lord, your God, re - turn
to the Lord, your God, who is grac - ious

and mer - ci - ful, slow to an - ger, and a - bound - ing in stead - fast love.

GOSPEL

The Gospel is announced.

℗ The Holy Gospel according to _____, the _____ chapter.
Ⓒ **Glory to you, O Lord.**

After the reading:

℗ The Gospel of the Lord.
Ⓒ **Praise to you, O Christ.**

Sit

SERMON

Silence for reflection may follow.

Stand

HYMN OF THE DAY

CREED

A Creed may be said: the Nicene Creed, on all festivals and on Sundays in the seasons of Advent/Christmas and Lent/Easter; the Apostles' Creed, at other times. When Holy Baptism or another rite with a creed is celebrated, this creed may be omitted.

NICENE CREED

Ⓒ **We believe in one God,**
    the Father, the Almighty,
    maker of heaven and earth,
    of all that is, seen and unseen.

We believe in one Lord, Jesus Christ,
    the only Son of God,
    eternally begotten of the Father,
    God from God, Light from Light,
    true God from true God,
    begotten, not made,
    of one Being with the Father.
    Through him all things were made.

For us and for our salvation
he came down from heaven;
by the power of the Holy Spirit
he became incarnate from the virgin Mary, and was made man.
For our sake he was crucified under Pontius Pilate;
he suffered death and was buried.
On the third day he rose again
in accordance with the Scriptures;
he ascended into heaven
and is seated at the right hand of the Father.
He will come again in glory to judge the living and the dead,
and his kingdom will have no end.

We believe in the Holy Spirit, the Lord, the giver of life,
who proceeds from the Father and the Son.
With the Father and the Son he is worshiped and glorified.
He has spoken through the prophets.
We believe in one holy catholic and apostolic Church.
We acknowledge one Baptism for the forgiveness of sins.
We look for the resurrection of the dead,
and the life of the world to come. Amen

APOSTLES' CREED

C I believe in God, the Father almighty,
creator of heaven and earth.

I believe in Jesus Christ, his only Son, our Lord.
He was conceived by the power of the Holy Spirit
and born of the virgin Mary.
He suffered under Pontius Pilate,
was crucified, died, and was buried.
He descended into hell.*
On the third day he rose again.
He ascended into heaven,
and is seated at the right hand of the Father.
He will come again to judge the living and the dead.

I believe in the Holy Spirit,
the holy catholic Church,
the communion of saints,
the forgiveness of sins,
the resurrection of the body,
and the life everlasting. Amen

*Or, He descended to the dead.

Stand/Kneel

THE PRAYERS

The Prayers begin with these or similar words:

Ⓐ Let us pray for the whole people of God in Christ Jesus, and for all people according to their needs.

Prayers are included for the whole Church, the nations, those in need, the parish, and special concerns. The congregation may be invited to offer other petitions. The minister gives thanks for the faithful departed, especially for those who recently have died.

Each portion of the prayers concludes with these or similar words:

OR

Ⓐ Lord, in your mercy,	Ⓐ Hear us, O God;
Ⓒ **hear our prayer.**	Ⓒ **your mercy is great.**

The prayers conclude with these or similar words:

Ⓟ Into your hands, O Lord, we commend all for whom we pray, trusting in your mercy; through your Son, Jesus Christ our Lord.
Ⓒ **Amen**

MEAL

Stand

PEACE

The Peace is shared.

Ⓟ The peace of the Lord be with you always.
Ⓒ **And also with you.**

The ministers and congregation may greet one another with a gesture of peace, using these or similar words: **Peace be with you.**

Sit

PRESENTATION OF THE GIFTS

The Offering is received as the Lord's Table is prepared.

The appointed Offertory may be sung by the choir as the gifts are presented, or the congregation may sing the following offertory, or an appropriate hymn or psalm may be sung.

Stand

Let the vine-yards be fruit-ful, Lord, and fill to the brim our cup of bless-ing. Gath-er a har-vest from the seeds that were sown, that we may be fed with the bread of life. Gath-er the hopes and dreams of all; u-nite them with the prayers we of-fer now. Grace our ta-ble with your pres-ence, Lord, and give us a fore-taste of the feast to come.

After the gifts have been presented, one of these prayers or another offertory prayer is said.

Ⓐ Let us pray.

Ⓐ Blessed are you,
Ⓒ **O Lord our God,**
maker of all things.
Through your goodness
you have blessed us with these gifts.
With them we offer ourselves
to your service
and dedicate our lives
to the care and redemption
of all that you have made,
for the sake of him
who gave himself for us,
Jesus Christ our Lord. Amen (240)

OR

Ⓐ Let us pray.

Ⓐ Merciful God,
Ⓒ **we offer with joy and thanksgiving**
what you have first given us —
our selves,
our time,
and our possessions,
signs of your gracious love.
Receive them
for the sake of him
who offered himself for us,
Jesus Christ our Lord. Amen (239)

GREAT THANKSGIVING

The Great Thanksgiving is begun by the presiding minister.

Ⓟ The Lord be with you.

Ⓒ **And also with you.**

Ⓟ Lift up your hearts.

Ⓒ **We lift them to the Lord.**

Ⓟ Let us give thanks to the Lord our God.

Ⓒ **It is right to give our thanks and praise.**

Ⓟ It is indeed right and salutary that we should at all times and in all places offer thanks... *(Here the minister continues with the proper preface, concluding:)* we praise your name and join their unending hymn:

Ⓒ Ho - ly, ho - ly, ho - ly Lord, God of pow-er and might, heav - en and earth are full of your glo - ry. Ho - san - na in the high - est. Bless-ed is he who comes in the name of the Lord. Ho - san - na in the high - est. Ho - san - na in the high - est.

The minister continues, using one of the prayers below.

OR

P We give you thanks, Father,
through Jesus Christ,
your beloved Son,
whom you sent in this end of the ages
to save and redeem us
and to proclaim to us your will.

He is your Word,
inseparable from you.
Through him you created all things,
and in him you take delight.
He is your Word,
sent from heaven to a virgin's womb.
He there took on our nature
and our lot
and was shown forth as your Son,
born of the Holy Spirit
and of the virgin Mary.

It is he,
our Lord Jesus,
who fulfilled all your will
and won for you a holy people;
he stretched out his hands in suffering
in order to free from suffering
those who trust you.

It is he
who, handed over to a death
he freely accepted,
in order to destroy death,
to break the bonds of the evil one,
to crush hell underfoot,
to give light to the righteous,
to establish his covenant,
and to show forth the resurrection,
taking bread and
giving thanks to you, said:
Take and eat;
this is my body,
broken for you.
Do this for the remembrance of me.

This prayer continues on page 38.

P Holy, mighty, and merciful Lord,
heaven and earth are full of your glory.
In great love you sent to us Jesus,
your Son, who reached out
to heal the sick and suffering,
who preached good news to the poor,
and who, on the cross,
opened his arms to all.

In the night in which he was betrayed,
our Lord Jesus took bread,
and gave thanks; broke it,
and gave it to his disciples,
saying: Take and eat;
this is my body, given for you.
Do this for the remembrance of me.

Again, after supper,
he took the cup, gave thanks,
and gave it for all to drink,
saying: This cup is
the new covenant in my blood,
shed for you and for all people
for the forgiveness of sin.
Do this for the remembrance of me.

Remembering, therefore,
his death, resurrection, and ascension,
we await his coming in glory.

Pour out your Holy Spirit,
that by this Holy Communion
we may know the unity
we share with all your people
in the body of your Son,
Jesus Christ our Lord.

Through him, with him, in him,
in the unity of the Holy Spirit,
all glory and honor is yours,
almighty Father, now and forever.
C **Amen**

The Lord's Prayer follows on page 39.

In the same way
   he took the cup,
   gave thanks,
   and gave it for all to drink, saying:
This is my blood poured out for you.
Do this for the remembrance of me.

Remembering, then,
   his death and resurrection,
   we lift this bread and cup before you,
   giving you thanks that
   you have made us worthy
   to stand before you
   and to serve you
   as your priestly people.

And we ask you:
   Send your Spirit
   upon these gifts of your Church;
   gather into one all who share this bread and wine;
   fill us with your Holy Spirit
   to establish our faith in truth,
   that we may praise and glorify you
   through your Son Jesus Christ.

Through him
   all glory and honor is yours,
   Almighty Father,
   with the Holy Spirit,
   in your holy Church
   both now and forever.

A - men, a - men, a - men, a - men, a - men.

LORD'S PRAYER

℣ Let us pray with confidence
in the words our Savior gave us:

℟ **Our Father in heaven,**
    hallowed be your name,
    your kingdom come,
    your will be done,
        on earth as in heaven.
  Give us today our daily bread.
  Forgive us our sins
    as we forgive those
        who sin against us.
  Save us from the time of trial
    and deliver us from evil.
  For the kingdom, the power,
    and the glory are yours,
    now and for ever. Amen

℣ Lord, remember us in your
kingdom, and teach us to pray:

℟ **Our Father, who art in heaven,**
    hallowed be thy name,
    thy kingdom come,
    thy will be done,
        on earth as it is in heaven.
  Give us this day our daily bread;
  and forgive us our trespasses,
    as we forgive those
        who trespass against us;
  and lead us not into temptation,
    but deliver us from evil.
  For thine is the kingdom,
    and the power, and the glory,
    forever and ever. Amen

Sit

COMMUNION

The communion follows. The bread may be broken for distribution.

As the ministers give the bread and cup to each communicant, they say these words:

The body of Christ, given for you. The blood of Christ, shed for you.
The communicant may say: **Amen**

As the people commune, hymns and other music may be used, and may include the following:

℟ Lamb of God, you take a-way the sin of the world; have mer-cy on us. Lamb of God, you take a-way the sin of the world; have mer-cy on us. Lamb of God, you take a-way the sin of the world; grant us peace, grant us peace.

Stand

After all have returned to their places, the minister may say these or similar words.

P The body and blood of our Lord Jesus Christ strengthen you and keep you in his grace.

C **Amen**

CANTICLE

A post-communion canticle or an appropriate hymn or song may be sung.

C Thank-ful hearts and voic - es raise; tell ev - 'ry -
one what God has done. Let all who seek the
Lord re - joice and bear Christ's ho - ly name.
Send us with your prom - is - es, O God,
and lead us forth in joy with shouts
of thanks-giv - ing. Al - le - lu - ia.
(Lent:) A - men, a - men.

PRAYER

The following or a similar post-communion prayer is said.

Ⓐ Let us pray.

Ⓐ Almighty God, you provide
the true bread from heaven,
your Son, Jesus Christ our Lord.
Grant that we who have received
the Sacrament of his body and blood
may abide in him and he in us,
that we may be filled with
the power of his endless life,
now and forever. (209)
Ⓒ **Amen**

Silence for reflection.

SENDING

BLESSING

The minister blesses the congregation, using this or another appropriate blessing.

Ⓟ Almighty God, Father, ☩ Son, and Holy Spirit,
bless you now and forever.
Ⓒ **Amen**

When there is a procession from the church, a hymn, song, or canticle may be sung.

DISMISSAL

The minister may dismiss the congregation.

Ⓐ Go in peace. Serve the Lord.
Ⓒ **Thanks be to God.**

HOLY COMMUNION
All Times and Places, Setting 6

GATHERING

An order for CONFESSION AND FORGIVENESS (p. 10) may precede this service.

HYMNS, SONGS, AND CANTICLES may be played and sung as the congregation and ministers gather.

With this or a similar biblical GREETING, the minister extends God's welcome.

Ⓟ The grace of our Lord Jesus Christ, the love of God,
and the communion of the Holy Spirit be with you all.

Ⓒ **And also with you.**

When a KYRIE is sung, one of the following or another appropriate litany may be used.

#601   Kyrie (Ghana)
#602   Kyrie (Russia)
#603   Holy God (Trisagion)
#604   Kyrie (Plainsong)
#605   Señor, ten piedad (Caribbean)

When a HYMN OF PRAISE is sung, one of the following or another appropriate hymn, song, or canticle may be used.

#606   Glory to God (*Liturgy of Joy*)
#607   Glory to God (*Mass of Creation*)
#608   This is the Feast of Victory (North America)
#787   Glory to God, We Give You Thanks (Great Britain)
#791   Alabaré (Central America)

The PRAYER OF THE DAY is said, and the congregation responds, **Amen.**

WORD

The Scripture READINGS for the day are proclaimed. Silence for reflection may follow each reading.

The PSALM is sung or said after the first reading.

When a GOSPEL ACCLAMATION is sung, one of the following or another appropriate hymn, song, or canticle may be used.

   #609   Hallelujah/Heleluyan (Native America)
   #610   Alleluia (South Africa)
   #611a Gospel Acclamation: *General* (Plainsong)
   #611b Gospel Acclamation: *Lent* (Plainsong)
   #612   Halle, Halle, Hallelujah (Caribbean)
   #613   Celtic Alleluia (North America)
   #614   Praise to You, O Christ, Our Savior (Lent)
   #615   Return to the Lord (Lent)

The GOSPEL is proclaimed.

The minister announces the Gospel:

Ⓟ The Holy Gospel according to _____, the _____ chapter.
Ⓒ **Glory to you, O Lord.**

After the reading:

Ⓟ The Gospel of the Lord.
Ⓒ **Praise to you, O Christ.**

The SERMON follows. Silence for reflection may follow the sermon.

The HYMN OF THE DAY, a song, or canticle is sung.

A CREED may be said: the Nicene Creed (p. 32 or 54), on all festivals and on Sundays in the seasons of Advent/Christmas and Lent/Easter; the Apostles' Creed (p. 33 or 55), at other times.

THE PRAYERS for the Church, the nations, those in need, the parish, and special concerns are offered, including thanks for the faithful departed.

Each portion of the prayers concludes with these or similar words:

	OR
Ⓐ Lord, in your mercy,	Ⓐ Hear us, O God;
Ⓒ **hear our prayer.**	Ⓒ **your mercy is great.**

The minister concludes the prayers, and the congregation responds, **Amen.**

MEAL

The PEACE is shared.

Ⓟ The peace of the Lord be with you always.

Ⓒ **And also with you.**

The ministers and congregation may greet one another with a gesture of peace, using these or similar words: **Peace be with you.**

The OFFERING is received as the Lord's Table is prepared.

During the PRESENTATION OF THE GIFTS, one of the following or another appropriate hymn, song, or canticle may be sung.

#705	As the Grains of Wheat
#732	Create in Me a Clean Heart
#758	Come to Us, Creative Spirit
#759	Accept, O Lord, the Gifts We Bring
#760	For the Fruit of All Creation
#761	Now We Offer

This or a similar offertory prayer may be said after the gifts have been presented.

Ⓐ Let us pray.

Ⓐ Blessed are you,

Ⓒ **O Lord, our God, maker of all things.**

Through your goodness you have blessed us with these gifts.

With them we offer ourselves to your service and dedicate our lives

to the care and redemption of all that you have made,

for the sake of him who gave himself for us, Jesus Christ our Lord. Amen (240)

The GREAT THANKSGIVING is begun by the presiding minister.

Ⓟ The Lord be with you.

Ⓒ **And also with you.**

Ⓟ Lift up your hearts.

Ⓒ **We lift them to the Lord.**

Ⓟ Let us give thanks to the Lord our God.

Ⓒ **It is right to give our thanks and praise.**

The Great Thanksgiving continues, using one of the eucharistic prayers provided in the leaders edition. The congregation responds to a seasonal preface with "Holy, holy, holy Lord," using one of the following or another appropriate setting.

#616	Holy, holy, holy Lord (*Land of Rest*)
#617	Holy, holy, holy Lord (*Deutsche Messe*)
#618	Holy, holy, holy Lord (North America)
#619	Holy, holy, holy Lord (*Mass of Creation*)

The minister continues the prayer of thanksgiving, remembering God's mighty deeds of salvation in creation and especially in the person of Jesus Christ. After remembering Jesus' word of promise and his command to celebrate this meal, the congregation may say or sing this acclamation of faith:

P …we proclaim the Lord's death until he comes.

C **Christ has died. Christ is risen. Christ will come again.**

The minister continues the prayer of thanksgiving by remembering the death and resurrection of Jesus and by praying for the presence of the Holy Spirit.

At the conclusion of the prayer, the congregation responds, **Amen.**

All join together in praying the LORD'S PRAYER (p. 39 or 56).

After the bread is broken, the COMMUNION is shared.

When music is used during communion, one of the following or other appropriate hymns, songs, and canticles may be sung.

#620   Agnus Dei (Plainsong)
#621   Lamb of God (North America)
#622   Lamb of God (North America)

While the table is being cleared after the communion, one of the following or another appropriate hymn, song, or CANTICLE may be sung.

#623   Thankful Hearts and Voices Raise (*Liturgy of Joy*)
#624   Now, Lord, You Let Your Servant Go in Peace (*Detroit Folk Mass*)
#625   Now, Lord, You Let Your Servant Go in Peace (North America)
#722   Hallelujah! We Sing Your Praises (South Africa)
#754   Let Us Talents and Tongues Employ (Caribbean)
#801   Thine the Amen, Thine the Praise (North America)

A PRAYER concludes the meal, and the congregation responds, **Amen.**

SENDING

The minister says a BLESSING.

P Almighty God, Father, ☩ Son, and Holy Spirit, bless you now and forever.

C **Amen**

With a DISMISSAL, the congregation is sent out in mission.

A Go in peace. Serve the Lord.

C **Thanks be to God.**

SERVICE OF WORD AND PRAYER

The leader may announce the day and its significance before the Gathering Song or before the readings.

Stand

GATHERING SONG

GREETING

The leader greets the congregation.

Ⓛ The grace of our Lord Jesus Christ, the love of God, and the communion of the Holy Spirit be with you all.
Ⓒ **And also with you.**

2 Corinthians 13:13

Advent to Transfiguration	*Lent to Pentecost*	*Season after Pentecost*
Ⓛ In the beginning was the Word, **Ⓒ and the Word was with God, and the Word was God.** Ⓛ In the Word was life, **Ⓒ and the life was the light of all people.** Ⓛ The Word became flesh and lived among us, **Ⓒ and we have seen his glory, full of grace and truth.**	Ⓛ The word is near you, **Ⓒ on your lips and in your heart.** Ⓛ If you confess with your lips that Jesus is Lord, **Ⓒ and believe in your heart that God raised him from the dead, you will be saved.** Ⓛ Faith comes from what is heard, **Ⓒ and what is heard comes through the word of Christ.**	Ⓛ You are the treasured people of the LORD, **Ⓒ a people holy to the LORD our God.** Ⓛ Keep the words of the LORD in your heart; teach them to your children. **Ⓒ Talk about them when you are at home and when you are away, when you lie down and when you rise.** Ⓛ One does not live by bread alone, **Ⓒ but by every word that comes from the mouth of the LORD.**
John 1	Romans 10	Deuteronomy 26, 11, 8

SCRIPTURE SONG

This canticle or another scripture song or hymn may be sung.

Refrain

C Sal - va - tion be - longs to our God and to Christ the Lamb for - ev - er and ev - er.

I Great and won-der-ful are your deeds, O God of the u - ni - verse; just and true are your ways, O Rul - er of all the na - tions.

Refrain

Who can fail to hon-or you, Lord, and sing the glo - ry of your name?

II For you a - lone are the Ho - ly One. All na - tions will draw near and wor - ship be - fore you,

Refrain

for your just and ho - ly works have been re - vealed.

Revelation 7:10, 15:3–4

PRAYER OF THE DAY

The salutation may precede the prayer.

L The Lord be with you.
C **And also with you.**

L Let us pray. *(The Prayer of the Day is said, concluding:)*
C **Amen**

WORD

Sit

READINGS

The scriptures appointed for the day are read. Psalms, hymns, songs, or anthems may be sung in response.

Before each reading, the reader may say: A reading from _____.
After each reading, the reader may say: The word of the Lord.
All may respond: **Thanks be to God.**

Stand

GOSPEL ACCLAMATION

This acclamation or a hymn, song, or canticle may be sung before and/or after the Gospel:

Ⓒ Word of life, Je - sus Christ, all glo - ry to you!

Word of life, Je - sus Christ, all praise to you!

Our hearts burn with - in us while you o - pen to us the Scrip-tures.

Word of life, Je - sus Christ, all glo - ry to you!

Word of life, Je - sus Christ, all praise to you!

GOSPEL

The Gospel is announced.

Ⓛ The Holy Gospel according to _____, the _____ chapter.
Ⓒ **Glory to you, O Lord.**

After the reading:

Ⓛ The Gospel of the Lord.
Ⓒ **Praise to you, O Christ.**

Sit

SERMON

Silence for reflection may follow.

Stand

RESPONSE TO THE WORD

A song, hymn, or canticle is sung.

As the singing concludes, the leaders may gather near the baptismal font. The response to the Word continues:

Ⓛ In Christ, you have heard the word of truth, the gospel of your salvation.
Ⓒ **We believe in him and are marked with the seal of the promised Holy Spirit.**

Ephesians 1:13–14

Ⓛ Living together in trust and hope, we confess our faith.
Ⓒ **I believe in God, the Father almighty,**
    creator of heaven and earth.

    I believe in Jesus Christ, his only Son, our Lord.
        He was conceived by the power of the Holy Spirit,
            and born of the virgin Mary.
        He suffered under Pontius Pilate,
            was crucified, died, and was buried.
        He descended into hell.*
        On the third day he rose again.
        He ascended into heaven,
            and is seated at the right hand of the Father.
        He will come again to judge the living and the dead.

    I believe in the Holy Spirit,
        the holy catholic Church,
        the communion of saints,
        the forgiveness of sins,
        the resurrection of the body,
        and the life everlasting. Amen

*Or, He descended to the dead.

Ⓛ Build yourselves up on your most holy faith;
Ⓒ **pray in the Holy Spirit.**

Jude 20

Ⓛ Keep yourselves in the love of God;
Ⓒ **look forward to the mercy of our Lord Jesus Christ.**

Jude 21

Ⓛ If anyone is in Christ, there is a new creation:
Ⓒ **Everything old has passed away;**
behold, everything has become new!

2 Corinthians 5:17

Ⓛ God has given us the ministry of reconciliation.
Therefore, let us be reconciled to God and to one another.

Kneel/Stand

Silence for reflection and self examination.

Ⓛ Gracious God,

Ⓒ **have mercy on us. In your compassion forgive us our sins,
known and unknown, things done and left undone.
Uphold us by your Spirit so that we may live and serve you in newness of life,
to the honor and glory of your holy name; through Jesus Christ our Lord. Amen**

The leader continues, using the appropriate section below.

OR

Ⓟ Almighty God
have mercy on you,
forgive you all your sins
through our Lord Jesus Christ,
strengthen you in all goodness,
and by the power of the Holy Spirit
keep you in eternal life.
Ⓒ **Amen**

Ⓛ The almighty and merciful Lord
grant us pardon, forgiveness,
and remission of all our sins.
Ⓒ **Amen**

Stand
PEACE

Ⓛ Sisters and brothers, rejoice. Mend your ways, encourage one another,
agree with one another, live in peace.   2 Corinthians 13:11

Ⓛ The peace of the Lord be with you always.
Ⓒ **And also with you.**

*The leaders and congregation may greet one another with a gesture of peace using these or
similar words:* **Peace be with you.**

PRAYER

Sit
OFFERING

An offering is received. Songs, hymns, canticles, and anthems may be played or sung.

Stand
OFFERTORY

*As the gifts are presented, the congregation may sing this Offertory or another appropriate
song, hymn, or canticle.*

Ⓒ *(Advent to Transfiguration)* **Glo - ry** to **you,** **God,** for **yours** is the **earth;**
(Lent to Pentecost) **Glo - ry** to **you,** **God,** for **yours** is the **earth;**
(Season after Pentecost) **Glo - ry** to **you,** **God,** for **yours** is the **earth;**

yours is the prom - ise, the bless - ing, the birth.
yours the ho - san - nas, the dy - ing, re - birth.
yours the a - noint - ing, the ra - di - ant worth.

Ours the re - joic - ing for Word giv - en frame;
Ours the re - joic - ing for na - ture re - claimed;
Ours the re - joic - ing for spir - its a - flame;

ours the thanks - giv - ing to your ho - ly name.

Ours be the tell - ing of deeds great - ly done;

yours be the glo - ry, O God, yours a - lone.

At the conclusion of the Offertory, one of these prayers or another offertory prayer may be said.

Advent to Transfiguration	*Lent to Pentecost*	*Season after Pentecost*
Ⓛ Let us pray.	Ⓛ Let us pray.	Ⓛ Let us pray.
Ⓛ Merciful God, **Ⓒ in the mystery of the Word made flesh, you embrace our lives with your great love for humanity. With joy and gladness we ask that these gifts may be for many a sign of that love, and that we may continue to share in your divine life, through Jesus Christ our Lord. Amen** (575)	Ⓛ Gracious God, **Ⓒ in the abundance of your steadfast love, you call us from death to life, from silence to speech, from idleness to action. With these gifts we offer ourselves to you, and with the Church through all the ages we give thanks for your saving love in Jesus Christ our Lord. Amen** (576)	Ⓛ God, our Creator, **Ⓒ you open wide your hand and satisfy the desire of every living creature. With these gifts we bless you for your tender nurture and care. Help us to delight in your will and walk in your ways, through Jesus Christ our Lord. Amen** (577)

THE PRAYERS

The prayers begin with these or similar words:

L As God's people called to love one another,
let us pray for the needs of the Church, the human family, and all the world.

Prayers are included for the whole Church, the nations, those in need, the parish, and special concerns. The congregation may be invited to offer other petitions. The leader gives thanks for the faithful departed, especially for those who recently have died.

Each portion of the prayers concludes with these or similar words:

OR

L Hear us, O God;
C **your mercy is great.**

L God of mercy,
C **hear our prayer.**

The prayers conclude with these or similar words:

L All these things and whatever else you see that we need, grant us, O God, for the sake of Christ who died and rose again, and now lives and reigns with you and the Holy Spirit, one God, forever and ever.
C **Amen**

LORD'S PRAYER

L Let us pray with confidence in the words our Savior gave us:

C **Our Father in heaven,**
  hallowed be your name,
  your kingdom come,
  your will be done,
    on earth as in heaven.
  Give us today our daily bread.
  Forgive us our sins
    as we forgive those
      who sin against us.
  Save us from the time of trial
    and deliver us from evil.
  For the kingdom, the power,
    and the glory are yours,
    now and forever. Amen

L Lord, remember us in your kingdom, and teach us to pray:

C **Our Father, who art in heaven,**
  hallowed be thy name,
  thy kingdom come,
  thy will be done,
    on earth as it is in heaven.
  Give us this day our daily bread;
  and forgive us our trespasses,
    as we forgive those
      who trespass against us;
  and lead us not into temptation,
    but deliver us from evil.
  For thine is the kingdom,
    and the power, and the glory,
    forever and ever. Amen

BLESSING

The blessing of God is announced, using one of these or other appropriate words.

OR

Ⓟ Almighty God,
Father, ✛ Son, and Holy Spirit,
bless you now and forever.
Ⓒ Amen

Ⓛ May the God and Father of
our Lord Jesus Christ fill you
with every spiritual blessing.
Ⓒ Amen

Ⓛ May the God of faithfulness and
encouragement grant you to live
in harmony with one another,
in accordance with Christ Jesus.
Ⓒ Amen

Ⓛ May the God of hope fill you
with all joy and peace in believing,
so that you may abound in hope
by the power of the Holy Spirit.
Ⓒ Amen   Romans 15

SENDING SONG

A hymn, song, or canticle may be sung as the people are sent forth.

DISMISSAL

The leader may dismiss the congregation.

Ⓛ Go in peace. Serve the Lord.
Ⓒ Thanks be to God.

PRAYING TOGETHER
Ecumenical Texts
English Language Liturgical Consultation (1988)

KYRIE

Lord, have mercy.   Christ, have mercy.   Lord, have mercy.

GLORY TO GOD

Glory to God in the highest,
and peace to God's people on earth.

Lord God, heavenly King,
almighty God and Father,
    we worship you, we give you thanks,
    we praise you for your glory.

Lord Jesus Christ, only Son of the Father,
Lord God, Lamb of God,
you take away the sin of the world:
    have mercy on us;
you are seated at the right hand of the Father:
    receive our prayer.

For you alone are the Holy One,
you alone are the Lord,
you alone are the Most High,
    Jesus Christ,
    with the Holy Spirit,
    in the glory of God the Father. Amen

NICENE CREED

We believe in one God,
    the Father, the Almighty,
    maker of heaven and earth,
    of all that is, seen and unseen.

We believe in one Lord, Jesus Christ,
    the only Son of God,
    eternally begotten of the Father,
    God from God, Light from Light,

true God from true God,
begotten, not made,
of one Being with the Father;
through him all things were made.
For us and for our salvation
    he came down from heaven,
    was incarnate of the Holy Spirit and the Virgin Mary
    and became truly human.
    For our sake he was crucified under Pontius Pilate;
    he suffered death and was buried.
    On the third day he rose again
    in accordance with the Scriptures;
    he ascended into heaven
    and is seated at the right hand of the Father.
    He will come again in glory to judge the living and the dead,
    and his kingdom will have no end.

We believe in the Holy Spirit, the Lord, the giver of life,
    who proceeds from the Father and the Son,
    who with the Father and the Son is worshiped and glorified,
    who has spoken through the prophets.
    We believe in one holy catholic and apostolic Church.
    We acknowledge one baptism for the forgiveness of sins.
    We look for the resurrection of the dead,
        and the life of the world to come. Amen

APOSTLES' CREED

I believe in God, the Father almighty,
    creator of heaven and earth.

I believe in Jesus Christ, God's only Son, our Lord,
    who was conceived by the Holy Spirit,
    born of the Virgin Mary,
    suffered under Pontius Pilate,
    was crucified, died, and was buried;
    he descended to the dead.
    On the third day he rose again;
    he ascended into heaven,
    he is seated at the right hand of the Father,
    and he will come to judge the living and the dead.

I believe in the Holy Spirit,
    the holy catholic Church,
    the communion of saints,
    the forgiveness of sins,
    the resurrection of the body,
    and the life everlasting. Amen

THANKSGIVING

The Lord be with you.
  And also with you.
Lift up your hearts.
  We lift them to the Lord.
Let us give thanks to the Lord our God.
  It is right to give our thanks and praise.

Holy, holy, holy Lord, God of power and might,
heaven and earth are full of your glory.
  Hosanna in the highest.
Blessed is he who comes in the name of the Lord.
  Hosanna in the highest.

OUR FATHER

Our Father in heaven,
  hallowed be your name,
  your kingdom come,
  your will be done,
    on earth as in heaven.
Give us today our daily bread.
Forgive us our sins
  as we forgive those who sin against us.
Save us from the time of trial
  and deliver us from evil.
For the kingdom, the power, and the glory are yours
  now and for ever. Amen

LAMB OF GOD

Lamb of God, you take away the sin of the world, have mercy on us.
Lamb of God, you take away the sin of the world, have mercy on us.
Lamb of God, you take away the sin of the world, grant us peace.

CANTICLE

Now, Lord, you let your servant go in peace:
  your word has been fulfilled.
My own eyes have seen the salvation
  which you have prepared in the sight of every people:
a light to reveal you to the nations
  and the glory of your people Israel.

SERVICE MUSIC, HYMNS, AND SONGS

Kyrie

601

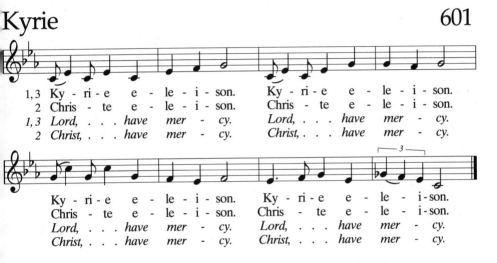

1,3 Ky - ri - e   e - le - i - son.   Ky - ri - e   e - le - i - son.
2   Chris - te   e - le - i - son.   Chris - te   e - le - i - son.
1,3 *Lord,* . . . *have   mer - cy.*   *Lord,* . . . *have   mer - cy.*
2   *Christ,* . . . *have   mer - cy.*   *Christ,* . . . *have   mer - cy.*

Ky - ri - e   e - le - i - son.   Ky - ri - e   e - le - i - son.
Chris - te   e - le - i - son.   Chris - te   e - le - i - son.
Lord, . . . *have   mer - cy.*   *Lord,* . . . *have   mer - cy.*
Christ, . . . *have   mer - cy.*   *Christ,* . . . *have   mer - cy.*

Music: Dinah Reindorf, Ghana, 20th cent.
Music © 1987 Dinah Reindorf

Pronunciation: kē-rē-ĕ (krēs-tĕ) ĕ-lĕ-ē-sŏn

Kyrie

602

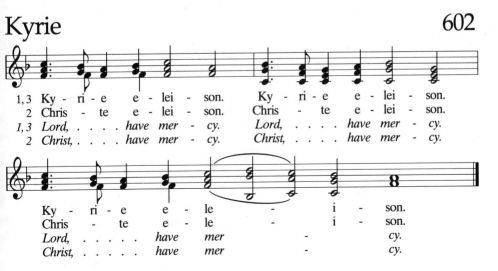

1,3 Ky - ri - e   e - lei - son.   Ky - ri - e   e - lei - son.
2   Chris - te   e - lei - son.   Chris - te   e - lei - son.
1,3 *Lord,* . . . . *have mer - cy.*   *Lord,* . . . . *have mer - cy.*
2   *Christ,* . . . . *have mer - cy.*   *Christ,* . . . . *have mer - cy.*

Ky - ri - e   e - le - i - son.
Chris - te   e - le - i - son.
Lord, ... *have mer - cy.*
Christ, ... *have mer - cy.*

Music: Russian Orthodox

Holy God
Trisagion

603

Ho-ly God, Ho-ly and Might-y, Ho-ly Im-mor-tal One, have mer-cy up-

on us. Ho-ly God, Ho-ly and Might-y, Ho-ly Im-mor-tal

One, have mer-cy up - on us. Ho-ly God, Ho-ly and Might-y,

Ho-ly Im-mor-tal One, have mer-cy up - on us, have mer-cy up-on us.

Text: Greek, tr. *Book of Common Prayer*
Music: *Music for the Eucharist*, David Hurd, b. 1950
Music © 1995 Augsburg Fortress

604

Kyrie

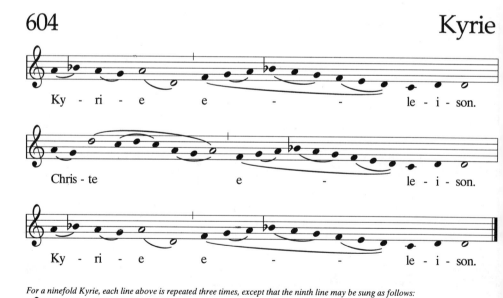

Ky - ri - e e - - le - i - son.

Chris - te e - le - i - son.

Ky - ri - e e - - le - i - son.

For a ninefold Kyrie, each line above is repeated three times, except that the ninth line may be sung as follows:

Ky - ri - e e - le - i - son.

Music: Plainsong, mode 1; Mass 11, *Orbis factor*

Señor, ten piedad
Lord, have mercy

A Se - ñor, ten pie - dad.
Lord, have mer - cy.
Have

C Se - ñor, ten pie-dad.
Lord, have mer - cy.

A Cris - to, ten pie - dad.
mer - cy on us, Christ.

C Cris - to, ten
Have mer - cy on

A Se - ñor, ten pie-dad.
Lord, have mer - cy.

pie - dad.
us, Christ.

C Se - ñor,
Lord,

A Se - ñor, ten pie-dad, Se - ñor.
Lord, have mer - cy, Lord.

ten pie-dad.
have mer - cy.

C ten pie-dad, Se - ñor.
have mer - cy, Lord.

Music: José Ruiz, b. 1956
Music © 1995 Augsburg Fortress

606

Glory to God

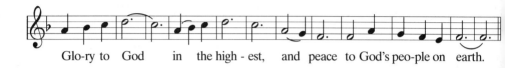

C Glo-ry to God in the high - est, and peace to God's peo-ple on earth.

Glo-ry to God in the high - est, and peace to God's peo-ple on earth.

I Lord God, heav-en-ly king, al - might-y God and Fa-ther, we wor-ship

you, we give you thanks, we praise you for your glo - ry.

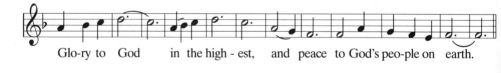

C Glo-ry to God in the high - est, and peace to God's peo-ple on earth.

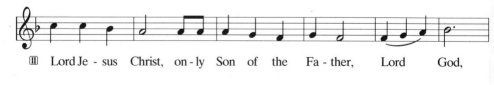

Glo-ry to God in the high - est, and peace to God's peo-ple on earth.

II Lord Je - sus Christ, on - ly Son of the Fa - ther, Lord God,

Lamb of God, you take a - way the sin of the world:

have mer - cy on us; you are seat - ed at the right

hand of the Fa - ther: re - ceive our prayer.

Glo-ry to God in the high - est, and peace to God's peo-ple on earth.

Glo-ry to God in the high - est, and peace to God's peo-ple on earth.

For you a - lone are the Ho - ly One, you a - lone are the

Lord, you a - lone are the Most High, Je - sus Christ, with the

Ho - ly Spir - it, in the glo - ry of God the Fa - ther.

Glo-ry to God in the high - est. A - men, a - men.

Music: *Liturgy of Joy,* James Capers, b. 1948
Music © 1993 Augsburg Fortress

607

Glory to God

C Glo - ry to God in the high - est, and peace to God's peo - ple on earth.

I Lord God, heav-en - ly king, al - might - y God and Fa - ther, we wor-ship you, we give you thanks, we praise you for your glo - ry.

C Glo - ry to God in the high - est, and peace to God's peo - ple on earth.

II Lord Je - sus Christ, on - ly Son of the Fa - ther, Lord God, Lamb of God, you take a - way the sin of the world: have mer - cy on us; you are seat - ed at the

Music: *Mass of Creation*, Marty Haugen, b. 1950
Music © 1984 GIA Publications, Inc.

608

This Is the Feast of Victory

This is the feast of vic - to - ry. Al - le - lu - ia, al - le - lu - ia. This is the feast of vic - to - ry. Al - le - lu - ia, al - le - lu - ia.

I Wor-thy is Christ, the Lamb who was slain, whose blood set us free to be peo - ple of God.

II Pow - er and rich - es and wis - dom and strength, and hon - or and bless - ing and glo - ry are his.

This is the feast of vic - to - ry. Al - le - lu - ia, al - le - lu - ia. This is the feast of

vic - to - ry. Al - le - lu - ia, al - le - lu - ia.

Ⅰ Sing with all the peo - ple of God, and

join in the hymn of all cre - a - tion:

Ⅱ Bless-ing and hon - or and glo - ry and might be to

God and the Lamb for - ev - er. A - men.

C This is the feast of vic - to - ry. Al - le - lu - ia,

al - le - lu - ia. For the Lamb who was slain has be -

gun his reign. Al - le - lu - ia, al - le - lu - ia.

Al - le - lu - ia, al - le - lu - ia.

Text: John W. Arthur, 1922–1980, based on Revelation 5
Music: Michael Hassell, b. 1952

Hallelujah
Heleluyan

609

Hal - le - lu - jah, hal - le - lu - jah; hal - le, hal - le - lu - jah;
He - le - lu - yan, he - le - lu - yan; he - le, he - le - lu - yan;

hal - le - lu - jah, hal - le - lu - jah; hal - le, hal - le - lu - jah.
he - le - lu - yan, he - le - lu - yan; he - le, he - le - lu - yan.

* may be sung in canon

Music: Muscogee (Creek) Indian; transcribed Charles Webb, b. 1933
Transcription © 1989 The United Methodist Publishing House

Alleluia

610

Al - le - lu - ia, al - le - lu - ia. Al - le - lu - ia, al - le - lu - ia.

Al - le - lu - ia, al - le - lu - ia. Al - le - lu - ia, al - le - lu - ia.

Music: South African; arr. Gobingca Mxadana, 20th cent.
Arr. © Gobingca Mxadana

Gospel Acclamation: *General*

611a

Al - le - lu - ia, al - le - lu - ia, al - le - lu - ia.

Music: Plainsong, mode 6

Gospel Acclamation: *Lent*

611b

Glo - ry and praise to you, O Lord Je - sus Christ.

Music: Plainsong, mode 1
Each Alleluia setting may be sung independently as an ostinato (repeated) refrain.
A proper Verse, when used, may be sung by a cantor or choir and inserted between two singings of the Alleluia setting.

Halle, Halle, Hallelujah 612

Hal - le, hal - le, hal - le - lu - jah!

Hal - le, hal - le, hal - le - lu - jah!
Hal - le - lu - jah!

Hal - le, hal - le, hal - le - lu - jah!

Hal - le - lu - jah! Hal - le - lu - jah!

Music: Caribbean traditional; arr. Mark Sedio, b. 1954
Arr. © 1995 Augsburg Fortress

Celtic Alleluia 613

Al - le - lu - ia, al - le - lu - ia!

Al - le - lu - ia, al - le - lu - ia!

Music: Fintan O'Carroll and Christopher Walker
Music © 1985 Fintan O'Carroll and Christopher Walker, admin. OCP Publications

614 Praise to You, O Christ, Our Savior

Refrain

Praise to you, O Christ, our Sav-ior, Word of the Fa-ther, call-ing us to life:

Son of God who leads us to free-dom; glo-ry to you, Lord Je-sus Christ!

1 You are the Word who calls us out of dark - ness;
2 You are the one whom proph-ets hoped and longed for;
3 You are the Word who calls us to be ser - vants;
4 You are the Word who binds us and u - nites us;

you are the Word who leads us in - to light; you are the Word who
you are the one who speaks to us to - day; you are the one who
you are the Word whose on - ly law is love; you are the Word made
you are the Word who calls us to be one; you are the Word who

Refrain

brings us through the des - ert: glo - ry to you, Lord Je - sus Christ!
leads us to our fu - ture: glo - ry to you, Lord Je - sus Christ!
flesh who lives a - mong us: glo - ry to you, Lord Je - sus Christ!
teach-es us for-give - ness: glo - ry to you, Lord Je - sus Christ!

Text: Bernadette Farrell, b. 1957
Music: Bernadette Farrell, b. 1957
© 1986 Bernadette Farrell, admin. OCP Publications

615 Return to the Lord

Re - turn to the Lord, your God, re - turn to the Lord your God, who is

gra-cious and mer-ci-ful, slow to an - ger, and a-bound-ing in stead-fast love.

Text: Joel 2:13
Music: Jay Beech, b. 1960
Music © 1995 Augsburg Fortress

Holy, Holy, Holy Lord

616a

Ho - ly, ho - ly, ho - ly Lord, God of pow - er and might:

heav'n and earth are full of your glo - ry. Ho - san - na in the high - est.

Bless - ed is he who comes in the name of the Lord.

Ho - san - na in the high - est, ho - san - na in the high - est.

Music: *Land of Rest,* American folk tune; adapt. Marcia Pruner
Adapt. © 1980 Church Pension Fund

Acclamations and Amen

616b

Christ has died. Christ is ris - en. Christ will come a - gain.

A - men, a - men. Come, Lord Je - sus, come.

A - men, a - men. Come, Ho - ly Spir - it, come.

A - men, a - men, a - men.

Music: *Land of Rest,* American folk tune

617a

Holy, Holy, Holy Lord

Ho - ly, ho - ly, ho - ly Lord, God of pow'r and might,

ho - ly, ho - ly, ho - ly Lord, God of pow'r and might:

heav-en and earth are full, full of your glo - ry.

Ho-san - na in the high - est, ho-san - na in the high - est.

Bless-ed is he who comes in the name of the Lord.

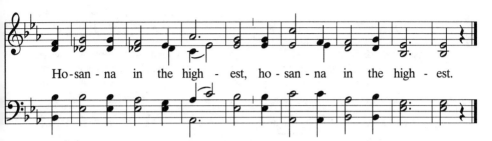

Ho-san - na in the high - est, ho-san - na in the high - est.

Music: *Deutsche Messe*, Franz Schubert, 1797–1828, adapt. Richard Proulx, b. 1937
Adapt. © 1985 GIA Publications, Inc.

Amen 617b

A - men, a - men, a - men. A - men, a - men.

Music: *Deutsche Messe*, Franz Schubert, 1797–1828, adapt.

Holy, Holy, Holy Lord 618a

Ho - ly, ho - ly, ho - ly Lord, God of pow-er and might:

heav'n and earth are full of your glo - ry. Ho - san - na

in the high - est, ho - san - na in the high - est. Bless-ed is

he who comes in the name of the Lord. Ho - san - na in the high - est.

Music: Michael Hassell, b. 1952
Music © 1995 Augsburg Fortress

618b — Acclamations and Amen

Christ has died. Christ is ris - en. Christ will come a - gain.
A - men. Come, Lord Je - sus. Come, Lord Je - sus, come.
A - men. Come, Ho-ly Spir - it. Ho - ly Spir - it, come.

A - men, a - men, a - men.

Music: Michael Hassell, b. 1952
Music © 1995 Augsburg Fortress

619a — Holy, Holy, Holy Lord

Ho-ly, ho - ly, ho - ly Lord, God of pow-er, God of might:

heav-en and earth are full of your glo-ry. Ho - san - na in the high-est.

Bless-ed is he who comes in the name of the Lord. Ho - san - na

in the high-est. Ho - san - na in the high - est.

Music: *Mass of Creation*, Marty Haugen, b. 1950
Music © 1984 GIA Publications, Inc.

619b — Acclamations and Amen

Christ has died. Christ is ris - en. Christ will come a - gain.

A - men, a - men. Come, Lord Je - sus, come.
A - men, a - men. Ho - ly Spir - it, come.

A - men, a - men, a - men.

Music: *Mass of Creation*, Marty Haugen, b. 1950
Music © 1984 GIA Publications, Inc.

Agnus Dei
Lamb of God

620

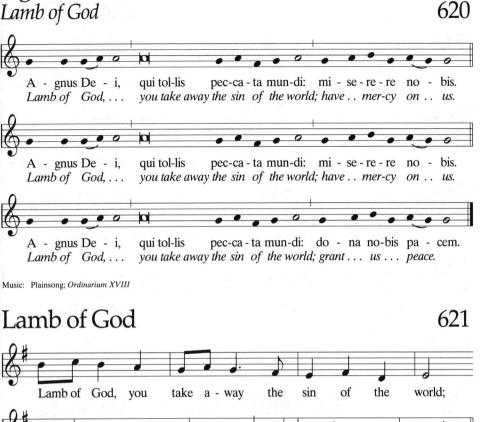

A - gnus De - i, qui tol-lis pec-ca - ta mun-di: mi - se - re - re no - bis.
Lamb of God, . . . you take away the sin of the world; have . . mer-cy on . . us.

A - gnus De - i, qui tol-lis pec-ca - ta mun-di: mi - se - re - re no - bis.
Lamb of God, . . . you take away the sin of the world; have . . mer-cy on . . us.

A - gnus De - i, qui tol-lis pec-ca - ta mun-di: do - na no-bis pa - cem.
Lamb of God, . . . you take away the sin of the world; grant . . . us . . . peace.

Music: Plainsong; *Ordinarium XVIII*

Lamb of God

621

Lamb of God, you take a - way the sin of the world;

have mer - cy on us, have mer - cy on us.

Lamb of God, you take a - way the sin of the world;

have mer - cy on us, have mer - cy on us.

Lamb of God, you take a - way the sin of the world;

grant us peace, grant us peace.

* May be sung in canon beginning here.
Music: Marty Haugen, b. 1950
Music © 1992 CPH Publishing

622 Lamb of God

Lamb of God, you take a-way the sin of the world; have mer-cy on us. Lamb of God, you take a-way the sin of the world; have mer-cy on us. Lamb of God, you take a-way the sin of the world; grant us peace, grant us peace, Lamb of God.

Music: Jay Beech, b. 1960
Music © 1995 Augsburg Fortress

623 Thankful Hearts and Voices Raise

Thank-ful hearts and voic-es raise; tell ev-'ry-one what God has done. Let all who seek the Lord re-joice and bear Christ's ho-ly name. Send us with your prom-is-es, O God, and lead us forth in joy with shouts of thanks-giv-ing. Al-le-lu - ia.
(Lent:) A - men, a - men.

Text: John Arthur, 1922–1980, alt., based on Ps. 105
Music: James Capers, b. 1948
Text © 1978, 1995 Augsburg Fortress
Music © 1993 Augsburg Fortress

Now, Lord,
You Let Your Servant Go in Peace

624

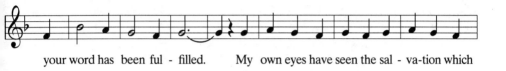

Now, Lord, you let your ser-vant go in peace;

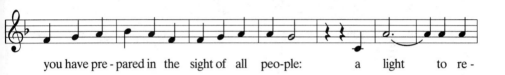

your word has been ful-filled. My own eyes have seen the sal-va-tion which

you have pre-pared in the sight of all peo-ple: a light to re-

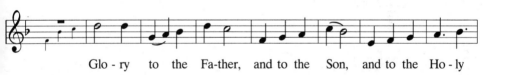

veal you to the na-tions and the glo-ry of your peo-ple Is-ra-el.

Glo-ry to the Fa-ther, and to the Son, and to the Ho-ly

Spir-it: as it was in the be-gin-ning, is now, and

will be for-ev-er. A - men

Music: *Detroit Folk Mass*, Tillis Butler and James Harris
Music © 1986 Fortress Press

Now, Lord,
625   You Let Your Servant Go in Peace

Now, Lord, you let your ser - vant go in peace;

your word has been ful - filled. My own eyes have seen the sal -

va - tion which you have pre - pared in the sight of ev - ery peo - ple:

a light to re - veal you to the na - tions and the glo - ry

of your peo - ple Is - ra - el.

Glo - ry to the Fa - ther, and to the Son, and to the Ho - ly

Spir - it: as it was in the be - gin - ning, is now, and

will be for - ev - er. A - men

Music: *Music for the Eucharist*, David Hurd, b. 1950
Music © 1995 Augsburg Fortress

People, Look East

626

1 Peo - ple, look east. The time is near of the crown-ing of the
2 Fur - rows, be glad. Though earth is bare, one more seed is plant-ed
3 Stars, keep the watch. When night is dim, one more light the bowl shall
4 An - gels an - nounce with shouts of mirth him who brings new life to

year. Make your house fair as you are a - ble, trim the
there. Give up your strength the seed to nour - ish, that in
brim, shin - ing be - yond the frost - y weath - er, bright as
earth. Set ev - 'ry peak and val - ley hum - ming with the

hearth and set the ta - ble.
course the flower may flour - ish. Peo - ple, look east, and sing to -
sun and moon to - geth - er.
word, the Lord is com - ing.

day—

Love, the Guest, is on the way.
Love, the Rose, is on the way.
Love, the Star, is on the way.
Love, the Lord, is on the way.

Text: Eleanor Farjeon, 1881–1965
Music: French carol, arr. Barry Rose, b. 1934
Text © 1931 Eleanor Farjeon, admin. David Higham Associates, Ltd.
Arr. © Barry Rose

BESANÇON
879887

627

My Lord, What a Morning

My Lord, what a morn-ing; my Lord, what a morn-ing; oh,
my Lord, what a morn-ing, when the stars be-gin to fall.

1 You'll hear the trum-pet sound,
2 You'll hear the sin - ner cry, to wake the na-tions un-der-ground,
3 You'll hear the Chris-tian shout,

look-ing to my God's right hand, when the stars be-gin to fall.

Text: African American spiritual
Music: African American spiritual

BURLEIGH
6 8 7 7 and refrain

Each Winter As the Year Grows Older 628

1 Each win-ter as the year grows old - er, we each grow old - er
2 When race and class cry out for trea - son, when si - rens call for
3 Yet I be-lieve be-yond be - liev - ing, that life can spring from
4 So e - ven as the sun is turn - ing to jour-ney to the
5 O Child of ec - sta - sy and sor - rows, O Prince of peace and

too. The chill sets in a lit - tle cold - er; the
war, they o - ver-shout the voice of rea - son and
death; that growth can flow - er from our griev - ing; that
north, the liv - ing flame, in se - cret burn - ing, can
pain, bright - en to - day's world by to - mor - row's, re -

ver - i - ties we knew seem shak - en and un - true.
scream till we ig - nore all we held dear be - fore.
we can catch our breath and turn trans-fixed by faith.
kin - dle on the earth and bring God's love to birth.
new our lives a - gain; Lord Je - sus, come and reign!

Text: William Gay, alt.
Music: Annabeth Gay, b. 1925
© 1971 United Church Press

CAROL OF HOPE
96966

All Earth Is Hopeful
Toda la tierra

629

1 All earth is hope - ful, the Sav - ior comes at last!
2 Peo - ple of Is - rael, you heard the proph - et tell:
3 Moun - tains and val - leys will have to be pre - pared;
4 We first saw Je - sus a ba - by in a crib.

Fur - rows lie o - pen for God's cre - a - tive task: this, the
"A vir - gin moth - er will bear Em - man - u - el"; she con -
new high-ways o - pened, new pro - to - cols de - clared. Al - most
This same Lord Je - sus to - day has come to live in our

la - bor of peo - ple who strug - gle to see how
ceived him, "God with us," our broth - er, whose birth re -
here! God is near - ing, in beau - ty and grace! All
world; he is pres - ent, in neigh - bors we see our

[1–3]

God's truth and jus - tice set ev - 'ry-bod-y free.
stores hope and cour - age to chil - dren of this earth.
clear ev - 'ry gate-way, in haste, come out in haste!
Je - sus is with us, and

[4]

ev-er sets us free.

1 *Toda la tierra espera al Salvador*
  y el surco abierto, la obra del Señor;
  es el mundo que lucha por la libertad,
  reclama justicia y busca la verdad.

2 *Dice el profeta al pueblo de Israel:*
  "De madre virgen ya viene Emmanuel,"
  será "Dios con nosotros," hermano será,
  con él la esperanza al mundo volverá.

3 *Montes y valles habrá que preparar;*
  nuevos caminos tenemos que trazar.
  Él está ya muy cerca, venidlo a encontrar,
  y todas las puertas abrid de par en par.

4 *En una cueva Jesús apareció,*
  pero en el mundo está presente hoy.
  Vive en nuestros hermanos, con ellos está;
  y vuelve de nuevo a darnos libertad.

Text: Alberto Taulé, b. 1932; tr. Madeleine Forell Marshall, b. 1946
Music: Alberto Taulé, b. 1932; arr. Skinner Chávez-Melo, b. 1944–1992
Text and tune © 1972 Alberto Taulé, admin. Virgil C. Funk
Tr. © 1995 Madeleine Forell Marshall, admin. Augsburg Fortress; arr. © Estate of Skinner Chávez-Melo

TAULÉ
11 11 12 12

Light One Candle to Watch for Messiah   630

1 Light one can-dle to watch for Mes-si - ah: let the light ban-ish dark - ness.
2 Light two can-dles to watch for Mes-si - ah: let the light ban-ish dark - ness.
3 Light three can-dles to watch for Mes-si - ah: let the light ban-ish dark - ness.
4 Light four can-dles to watch for Mes-si - ah: let the light ban-ish dark - ness.

He shall bring sal - va - tion to Is - ra-el, God ful - fills the prom - ise.
He shall feed the flock like a shep-herd, gent - ly lead them home - ward.
Lift your heads and lift high the gate-way for the King of glo - ry.
He is com - ing, tell the glad tid - ings. Let your lights be shin - ing!

Text: Wayne L. Wold, b. 1954
Music: Yiddish folk tune, arr. Wayne L. Wold, b. 1954
Text & Arr. © 1984 Fortress Press

TIF IN VELDELE
10 7 9 6

631 Lift Up Your Heads, O Gates

1 Lift up your heads, O gates; the King of
2 Who is this glo - rious King whose praise the
3 Lift up your heads, O gates; the King of
4 Sing ho - ly, ho - ly Lord, by heav'n and

glo - ry waits. Lift high, O an - cient doors, o - bey;
na - tions sing? The Lord, the Might - y, Ho - ly One,
glo - ry waits. Lift high, O an - cient doors, o - bey;
earth a - dored: O God of pow'r, O God of might,

Refrain

pre - pare the roy - al way.
whose strength the vic - t'ry won.
pre - pare the roy - al way.
you reign in glo - rious light. Ho - san - na,

ho - san - na! Re - joice, give thanks, and sing!

Text: Ps. 24:7–9, vers. Bert Polman, b. 1945, st. 1–3; *With One Voice*, st. 4
Music: Richard W. Dirksen, b. 1921
Text © 1987 CRC Publications, st. 1–3; © 1995 Augsburg Fortress, st. 4
Music © 1974 Harold Flammer Music, a division of Shawnee Press, Inc. (A.S.C.A.P.)

VINEYARD HAVEN
S M and refrain

The Angel Gabriel from Heaven Came 632

1 The an - gel Ga - bri - el from heav - en came,
2 "For know a bless - ed moth - er thou shalt be,
3 Then gen - tle Mar - y meek - ly bowed her head;
4 Of her, Em - man - u - el, the Christ, was born

with wings as drift - ed snow, with eyes as flame:
all gen - er - a - tions laud and hon - or thee;
"To me be as it pleas - eth God," she said.
in Beth - le - hem all on a Christ - mas morn,

"All hail to thee, O low - ly maid - en Mar - y,
thy son shall be Em - man - u - el, by seers fore - told,
"My soul shall laud and mag - ni - fy God's ho - ly name."
and Chris - tian folk through-out the world will ev - er say:

most high - ly fa - vored la - dy."
most high - ly fa - vored la - dy."
Most high - ly fa - vored la - dy,
"Most high - ly fa - vored la - dy,"

Glo - ri - a!

Text: Basque carol, para. Sabine Baring-Gould, 1834–1924
Music: Basque carol, arr. C. Edgar Pettman, 1865–1943, and John Wickham
Arr. © 1955 E.H. Freeman, Ltd., ren. 1983, admin. Glenwood Music Corp.

GABRIEL'S MESSAGE
10 10 12 10

633 Awake, Awake, and Greet the New Morn

1 A - wake! a - wake, and greet the new morn, for
2 To us, to all in sor - row and fear, Em -
3 In dark - est night his com - ing shall be, when
4 Re - joice, re - joice, take heart in the night, though

an - gels her - ald its dawn - ing. Sing out your joy, for
man - u - el comes a - sing - ing, his hum - ble song is
all the world is de - spair - ing, as morn - ing light so
dark the win - ter and cheer - less, the ris - ing sun shall

soon he is born, be - hold! the Child of our long - ing.
qui - et and near, yet fills the earth with its ring - ing;
qui - et and free, so warm and gen - tle and car - ing.
crown you with light, be strong and lov - ing and fear - less.

Come as a ba - by weak and poor, to bring all hearts to -
mu - sic to heal the bro - ken soul and hymns of lov - ing -
Then shall the mute break forth in song, the lame shall leap in
Love be our song and love our prayer and love our end - less

geth - er, he o - pens wide the heav'n - ly door and
kind - ness, the thun - der of his an - thems roll to
won - der, the weak be raised a - bove the strong, and
sto - ry; may God fill ev - 'ry day we share and

lives now in - side us for ev - er.
shat - ter all ha - tred and blind - ness.
weap-ons be bro - ken a - sun - der.
bring us at last in - to glo - ry.

Text: Marty Haugen, b. 1950
Music: Marty Haugen, b. 1950
© 1983 GIA Publications, Inc.

REJOICE, REJOICE
98988789

634 Sing of Mary, Pure and Lowly

1 Sing of Mar - y, pure and low - ly, vir - gin
2 Sing of Je - sus, son of Mar - y, in the
3 Glo - ry be to God the Fa - ther; glo - ry

moth-er, wise and mild. Sing of God's own Son most ho - ly, who be -
home at Naz - a - reth. Toil and la - bor can - not wea - ry love en -
be to God the Son; glo - ry be to God the Spir - it; glo - ry

came her lit - tle child. Fair - est child of fair - est moth - er, God the
dur - ing un - to death. Con-stant was the love he gave her, though he
to the Three in One. From the heart of bless-ed Mar - y, from all

Lord who came to earth, Word made flesh, our ver - y
went forth from her side, forth to preach, and heal, and
saints the song as - cends, and the Church the strain re -

broth - er,   takes   our   na - ture   by   his   birth.
suf - fer,   till   on   Cal - va - ry   he   died.
ech - oes   un - to   earth's re - mot - est   ends.

Text: Roland F. Palmer, 1891–1985
Music: Skinner Chávez-Melo, 1944–1992
Music © 1985 Estate of Skinner Chávez-Melo

RAQUEL
8 7 8 7 D

alt. tune: NETTLETON

Surely It Is God Who Saves Me   635

1   Surely it is God who saves me;
     I shall trust and have no fear.
   For the Lord defends and shields me
     and his saving help is near.
   So rejoice as you draw water
     from salvation's healing spring;
   in the day of your deliv'rance
     thank the Lord, his mercies sing.

2   Make God's deeds known to the peoples;
     tell out his exalted name.
   Praise the Lord, who has done great things;
     all his works God's might proclaim.
   Zion, lift your voice in singing;
     for with you has come to dwell,
   in your very midst, the great and
     Holy One of Israel.

Text: Carl P. Daw, Jr., b. 1944

© 1982, 1990 Hope Publishing Co.

RAQUEL
8 7 8 7 D

alt. tune: BEACH SPRING

636

Before the Marvel of This Night

1 Be - fore the mar - vel of this night, a - dor - ing,
2 A - wake the sleep - ing world with song, this is the
3 The love that we have al - ways known, our con - stant

fold your wings and bow, then tear the sky a - part with light
day the Lord has made. As - sem - ble here, ce - les - tial throng,
joy and end - less light, now to the love-less world be shown,

and with your news the world en - dow. Pro - claim the
in roy - al splen-dor come ar - rayed. Give earth a
now break up - on its death - ly night. In - to one

birth of Christ and peace, that fear and death and sor - row cease:
glimpse of heav'n - ly bliss, a teas - ing taste of what they miss:
song com - press the love that rules our u - ni - verse a - bove:

sing peace, sing peace, sing gift of
sing bliss, sing bliss, sing end - less
sing love, sing love, sing God is

peace, sing peace, sing gift of peace!
bliss, sing bliss, sing end - less bliss!
love, sing love, sing God is love!

Text: Jaroslav J. Vajda, b. 1919
Music: Carl Schalk, b. 1929
Text © 1981 Jaroslav J. Vajda
Tune © 1979 GIA Publications, Inc.
Arr. © 1982 Augsburg Publishing House

MARVEL
88888886

Gloria, Gloria, Gloria 637

Glo - ria, glo - ria, glo - ria, glo - ry be to God on high!
¡Glo - ria, glo - ria, glo - ria en las al - tur - as a Dios!

And on earth be peace to the peo-ple in whom God is well pleased.
Y en la tie - rra paz pa-ra a-que-llos . . . que a-ma el Se - ñor.

Text: Luke 2:14
Music: Pablo Sosa, Argentina, 20th cent.
Music © 1989 Pablo Sosa, admin. OCP Publications

GLORIA CUECA
irregular

Holy Child within the Manger

638

Carol at the Manger

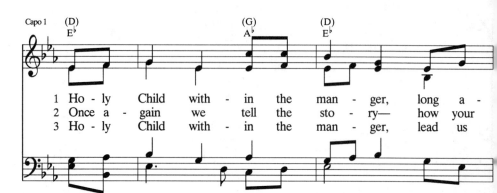

1 Ho - ly Child with - in the man - ger, long a -
2 Once a - gain we tell the sto - ry— how your
3 Ho - ly Child with - in the man - ger, lead us

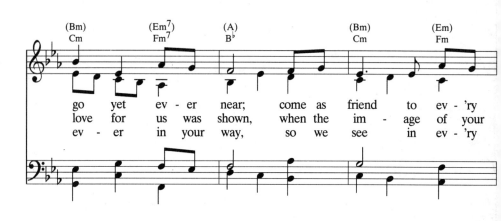

go yet ev - er near; come as friend to ev - 'ry
love for us was shown, when the im - age of your
ev - er in your way, so we see in ev - 'ry

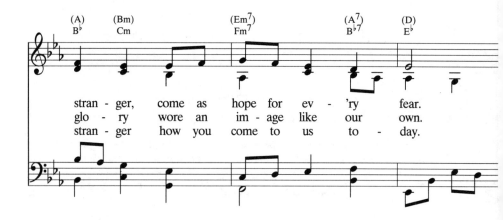

stran - ger, come as hope for ev - 'ry fear.
glo - ry wore an im - age like our own.
stran - ger how you come to us to - day.

Text: Marty Haugen, b. 1950
Music: Marty Haugen, b. 1950
© 1987 GIA Publications, Inc.

JOYOUS LIGHT
8 7 8 7 D

639 Oh, Sleep Now, Holy Baby

1 Oh, sleep now, ho - ly ba - by, with your head a - gainst my breast; ..
2 You need not fear King Her-od, he will bring no harm to you; so

mean-while the pangs of my sor - row are soothed and put to rest.
rest in the arms of your moth - er who sings you a la ru.

Refrain/Estribillo

*A la ru, a la mé, a la ru, a la mé,

* These are lullaby words with no specific meaning.

a la ru, a la mé, a la ru, a la ru, a la mé.

1 *Duérmete, Niño lindo, en los brazos del amor*
mientras que duerme y descansa la pena de mi dolor.   Estribillo

2 *No temas al rey Herodes que nada te ha de hacer;*
en los brazos de tu madre y ahi nadie te ha de ofender.   Estribillo

Text: Hispanic folk song; tr. John Donald Robb, 1892–1989
Music: Hispanic folk tune; arr. John Donald Robb, 1892–1989
Tr. and arr. © 1954 University of New Mexico Press

A LA RU
irregular

Gloria
Glory to God

640

Canon 1   2

Glo - ri - a,   glo - ri - a,   in ex - cel - sis De - o!
Glo-ry to God, glo - ry to God, glo - ry in the high - est!

3   4

Glo - ri - a,   glo - ri - a,   al - le - lu - ia, al - le - lu - ia!
Glo-ry to God, glo - ry to God, al - le - lu - ia, al - le - lu - ia!

Text: Traditional
Music: Jacques Berthier, 1923–1994
© 1979, 1988 Les Presses de Taizé, admin. GIA Publications, Inc.

GLORIA 3
irregular

641

Peace Came to Earth

1 Peace came to earth at last that cho - sen night
2 And who could be the same for hav - ing held
3 You show the Fa - ther none has ev - er seen,
4 How else could I have known you, O my God!

when an - gels clove the sky with song and light
the in - fant in their arms, and lat - er felt
in flesh and blood you bore our griefs and pains,
How else could I have loved you, O my God!

and God em - bod - ied love and sheathed his might—
the wound-ed hands and side, all doubts dis - pelled—
in bread and wine you vis - it us a - gain—
How else could I em - brace you, O my God!

Who could but gasp: Im - man - u - el!
Who could but sigh: Im - man - u - el!
Who could but see: Im - man - u - el!
Who could but pray: Im - man - u - el!

Who could but sing: Im - man - u - el!
Who could but shout: Im - man - u - el!
Who could but thrill: Im - man - u - el!
Who could but praise Im - man - u - el!

Text: Jaroslav J. Vajda, b. 1919
Music: Paul Manz, b. 1919
Text © 1984 Jaroslav J. Vajda
Music © 1991 Morning Star Music Publishers

SCHNEIDER
10 10 10 8 8

I Wonder As I Wander 642

1 I won - der as I wan - der, out un - der the sky, how
2 When Mar - y birthed . . . Je - sus, all in a cow's stall, came
3 If Je - sus had . . . want - ed for an - y wee thing, a
4 I won - der as I wan - der, out un - der the sky, how

Je - sus the Sav - ior did come for to die for poor ord' - n'ry peo - ple like
wise men and farm - ers and shep - herds and all, and high from the heav - ens a
star in the sky or a bird on the wing, or all of God's an - gels in
Je - sus the Sav - ior did come for to die for poor ord' - n'ry peo - ple like

you and like I. I won - der as I wan - der, out un - der the sky.
star's light did fall; the prom - ise of the a - ges it then did re - call.
heav'n for to sing, he sure - ly could have had it, 'cause he was the king.
you and like I. I won - der as I wan - der, out un - der the sky.

Text: Appalachian carol, collected by John Jacob Niles, 1892–1980
Music: Appalachian folk tune, adapt. John Jacob Niles, 1892–1980
© 1934 (renewed) by G. Schirmer, Inc. (A.S.C.A.P.)

I WONDER
12 11 11 12

643   Once in Royal David's City

1 Once in roy - al Da - vid's cit - y stood a low - ly cat - tle shed,
2 He came down to earth from heav-en who is God and Lord of all,
3 And our eyes at last shall see him, through his own re - deem-ing love;
4 Not in that poor low - ly sta - ble, with the ox - en stand-ing by,

where a moth - er laid her ba - by in a man - ger for his bed:
and his shel - ter was a sta - ble, and his cra - dle was a stall;
for that child so dear and gen - tle is our Lord in heav'n a - bove;
we shall see him; but in heav - en, set at God's right hand on high;

Mar - y was that moth - er mild, Je - sus Christ, her lit - tle child.
with the poor and meek and low-ly, lived on earth our Sav-ior ho - ly.
and he leads his chil - dren on to the place where he is gone.
there his chil - dren gath - er 'round, bright like stars, with glo - ry crowned.

Text: Cecil F. Alexander, 1818–1895
Music: Henry J. Gauntlett, 1805–1876

IRBY
878777

Away in a Manger

Text: USA, 19th cent.
Music: William J. Kirkpatrick, 1838–1921; arr. David Willcocks, b. 1919
arr. © 1960 Oxford University Press

CRADLE SONG
11 11 11 11

645 There's a Star in the East

1 There's a star in the East on Christ-mas morn, rise up, shep-herd, and fol-low.
2 If you take good heed to the an-gel's words, rise up, shep-herd, and fol-low.

It will lead to the place where the Christ was born, rise up, shep-herd, and fol-low.
You'll for-get your flocks, you'll for-get your herds, rise up, shep-herd, and fol-low.

Refrain

Fol - low, fol - low, rise up, shep-herd, and fol - low,

fol-low the star of Beth-le - hem, rise up, shep-herd, and fol-low.

Text: African American spiritual
Music: African American spiritual

RISE UP, SHEPHER
irregula

We Three Kings of Orient Are

646

1 We three kings of O-ri-ent are; bear-ing gifts we tra-verse a-
2 Born a king on Beth-le-hem's plain, gold I bring to crown him a-
3 Frank-in-cense to of-fer have I; in-cense owns a de-i-ty
4 Myrrh is mine; its bit-ter per-fume breathes a life of gath-er-ing
5 Glo-rious now be-hold him a-rise, King and God and Sac-ri-

far, field and foun-tain, moor and moun-tain, fol-low-ing yon-der star.
gain; king for-ev-er, ceas-ing nev-er, o-ver us all to reign.
nigh; prayer and prais-ing, glad-ly rais-ing, wor-ship-ing God Most High.
gloom; sor-row-ing, sigh-ing, bleed-ing, dy-ing, sealed in the stone-cold tomb.
fice; heav'n sings al-le-lu-ia: al-le-lu-ia the earth re-plies.

Refrain

Oh, star of won-der, star of night, star with roy-al beau-ty

bright; west-ward lead-ing, still pro-ceed-ing, guide us to thy per-fect light!

Text: John Henry Hopkins, Jr., 1820–1891, alt.
Music: John Henry Hopkins, Jr., 1820–1891

THREE KINGS OF ORIENT
8 8 4 4 6 and refrain

647 When Jesus Came to Jordan

1 When Je - sus came to Jor - dan to be bap-tized by John,
2 He came to share temp - ta - tion, our ut - most woe and loss,
3 Come, Ho - ly Spir - it, aid us to keep the vows we make;

he did not come for par - don but as the Sin - less One.
for us and our sal - va - tion to die up - on the cross.
this ver - y day in - vade us, and ev - 'ry bond-age break.

He came to share re - pen - tance with all who mourn their sins,
So when the dove de - scend - ed on him, the Son of Man,
Come, give our lives di - rec - tion, the gift we cov - et most:

to speak the vi - tal sen - tence with which good news be - gins.
the hid - den years had end - ed, the age of grace be - gan.
to share the res - ur - rec - tion that leads to Pen - te - cost.

Text: Fred Pratt Green, b. 1903
Music: English folk tune, adapt. Ralph Vaughan Williams, 1872–1958
Text © 1980 Hope Publishing Co.
Music © 1906 Oxford University Press

KING'S LYNN
7 6 7 6 D

alternate tune: AURELIA

Jesus, Come! For We Invite You

648

1 Je - sus, come! for we in - vite you, guest and mas - ter, friend and Lord; now, as once at Ca - na's wed - ding, speak and let us hear your word: lead us through our need or doubt - ing, hope be born and joy re - stored.

2 Je - sus, come! trans-form our plea - sures, guide us in - to paths un - known; bring your gifts, com-mand your ser - vants, let us trust in you a - lone: though your hand may work in se - cret, all shall see what you have done.

3 Je - sus, come! in new cre - a - tion, heav'n brought near in pow'r di - vine; give your un - ex - pect - ed glo - ry, chang-ing wa - ter in - to wine: rouse the faith of your dis - ci - ples— come, our first and great - est Sign!

4 Je - sus, come! sur - prise our dull - ness, make us will - ing to re - ceive more than we can yet im - ag - ine, all the best you have to give: let us find your hid - den rich - es, taste your love, be - lieve, and live!

Text: Christopher Idle, b. 1938
Music: Harold Friedell, 1905–1958
Text © 1982 Hope Publishing Co.
Music © 1957, 1985 H.W. Gray, admin. CPP/Belwin

UNION SEMINARY
878787

alt. tune: REGENT SQUARE

649   I Want to Walk as a Child of the Light

1 I want to walk as a child of the light.
2 I want to see ... the bright-ness of God.
3 I'm look-ing for ... the com-ing of Christ.

I want to fol - low Je - sus.
I want to look at Je - sus.
I want to be with Je - sus.

God set the stars to give light to the world.
Clear Sun of Righ - teous - ness, shine on my path,
When we have run .... with pa - tience the race,

The star of my life ... is Je - sus.
and show me the way to the Fa - ther.
we shall know the joy ... of Je - sus.

Refrain

In him there is no dark-ness at all.

The night and the day are both a-like.

The Lamb is the light of the cit-y of God.

Shine in my heart, Lord Je - sus.

HOUSTON
10 7 10 8 and refrain

We Are Marching in the Light of God
Siyahamba

We are march - ing* in the light of God, we are march-ing in the
Si - ya - hamb' e - ku - kha - nyen' kwen-khos', si - ya - hamb' e - ku - kha -

light of God. We are march - ing in the light of God,
nyen' kwen - khos'. Si - ya - hamb' e - ku - kha - nyen' kwen-khos',

si- ya - hamb' e - ku - kha - nyen' kwen - khos'.
we are march - ing in the light of God.

we are march - ing in the light of, the light of God.
si - ya - hamb' e - ku - kha - nyen' kwen-, kha - nyen' kwen - khos'.

we are march-ing in the light of God.
si - ya - hamb' e - ku - kha - nyen' kwen - khos'.

Si - ya - ham - ba   Oo
We are   march - ing   Oo

We are march - ing, march-ing, we are march-ing, march-ing,
Si - ya - ham - ba, ham - ba, si - ya - ham - ba, ham - ba,

alternate text: dancing, praying, singing

Text: South African
Music: South African
© 1984 Utryck, admin. Walton Music Corp.

SIYAHAMBA
irregular

651

Shine, Jesus, Shine

Shine, Je - sus, shine, fill this land with the Fa - ther's glo - ry;
blaze, Spir - it, blaze, set our hearts on fire.
Flow, riv - er, flow, flood the na - tions with love and mer - cy;
send forth your Word, Lord, and let there be light!

Text: Graham Kendrick
Music: Graham Kendrick
© 1987 Make Way Music, admin. (in Western Hemisphere) Integrity's Hosanna! Music

SHINE, JESUS, SHINE
9 9 10 10 3 3 and refrain

652 Arise, Your Light Has Come!

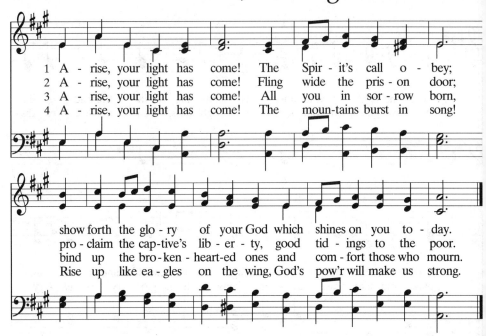

1 A - rise, your light has come! The Spir - it's call o - bey;
2 A - rise, your light has come! Fling wide the pris - on door;
3 A - rise, your light has come! All you in sor - row born,
4 A - rise, your light has come! The moun-tains burst in song!

show forth the glo - ry of your God which shines on you to - day.
pro - claim the cap-tive's lib - er - ty, good tid - ings to the poor.
bind up the bro - ken - heart-ed ones and com - fort those who mourn.
Rise up like ea - gles on the wing, God's pow'r will make us strong.

Text: Ruth Duck, b. 1947
Music: William H. Walter, 1825–1893
Text © 1992 GIA Publications, Inc.

FESTAL SONG
S M

653 Jesus on the Mountain Peak

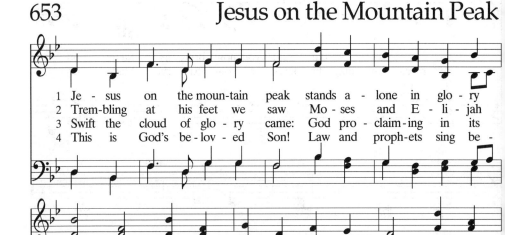

1 Je - sus on the moun-tain peak stands a - lone in glo - ry
2 Trem-bling at his feet we saw Mo - ses and E - li - jah
3 Swift the cloud of glo - ry came: God pro - claim-ing in its
4 This is God's be - lov - ed Son! Law and proph-ets sing be -

blaz - ing; let us, if we dare to speak, join the
speak - ing. All the proph - ets and the law shout through
thun - der Je - sus as the Son by name! Na - tions,
fore him, first and last and on - ly One. All cre -

saints and an - gels prais - ing. Al - le - lu - ia!
them their joy - ful greet - ing: Al - le - lu - ia!
cry a - loud in won - der: Al - le - lu - ia!
a - tion shall a - dore him! Al - le - lu - ia!

Text: Brian Wren, b. 1936
Music: Henry J. Gauntlett, 1805–1876
Text © 1977 by Hope Publishing Co.

ST. ALBINUS
78784

Alleluia, Song of Gladness 654

1 Al - le - lu - ia, song of glad - ness, voice of joy that can - not die;
2 Al - le - lu - ia! Lead our prais - es, true Je - ru - sa - lem and free;
3 Al - le - lu - ia can - not al - ways be our song while here be - low;
4 In our hymns we pray with long - ing: Grant us, bless - ed Trin - i - ty,

al - le - lu - ia is the an - them ev - er dear to choirs on high;
al - le - lu - ia, joy - ful moth-er, bring us to your ju - bi - lee;
al - le - lu - ia our trans-gres-sions make us for a while for - go;
at the last to keep glad Eas - ter with the faith-ful saints on high;

in the house of God a - bid - ing thus they sing e - ter - nal - ly.
but by Bab - y - lon's sad wa - ters mourn-ing ex - iles now are we.
for the sol - emn time is com - ing when our tears for sin shall flow.
there to you for - ev - er sing - ing al - le - lu - ia joy - ful - ly.

Text: Latin hymn, 11th cent.; tr. John M. Neale, 1818–1866, alt.
Music: John Goss, 1800–1880

PRAISE, MY SOUL
878787

655 As the Sun with Longer Journey

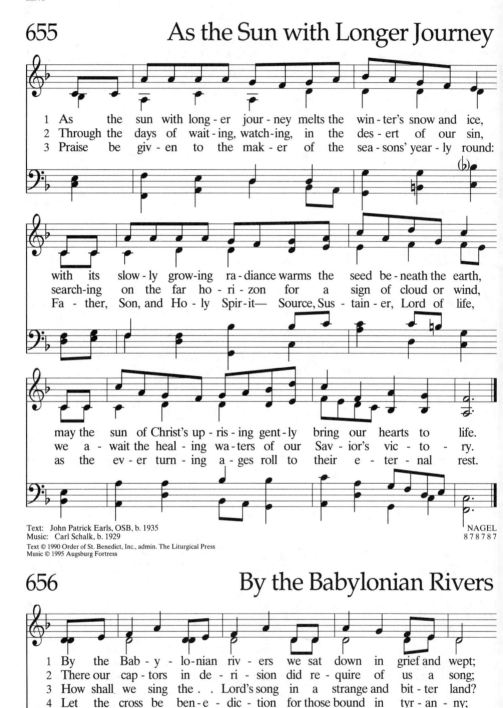

1 As the sun with long-er jour-ney melts the win-ter's snow and ice,
2 Through the days of wait-ing, watch-ing, in the des-ert of our sin,
3 Praise be giv-en to the mak-er of the sea-sons' year-ly round:

with its slow-ly grow-ing ra-diance warms the seed be-neath the earth,
search-ing on the far ho-ri-zon for a sign of cloud or wind,
Fa-ther, Son, and Ho-ly Spir-it— Source, Sus-tain-er, Lord of life,

may the sun of Christ's up-ris-ing gent-ly bring our hearts to life.
we a-wait the heal-ing wa-ters of our Sav-ior's vic-to-ry.
as the ev-er turn-ing a-ges roll to their e-ter-nal rest.

Text: John Patrick Earls, OSB, b. 1935
Music: Carl Schalk, b. 1929

NAGEL
878787

Text © 1990 Order of St. Benedict, Inc., admin. The Liturgical Press
Music © 1995 Augsburg Fortress

656 By the Babylonian Rivers

1 By the Bab-y-lo-nian riv-ers we sat down in grief and wept;
2 There our cap-tors in de-ri-sion did re-quire of us a song;
3 How shall we sing the . . Lord's song in a strange and bit-ter land?
4 Let the cross be ben-e-dic-tion for those bound in tyr-an-ny;

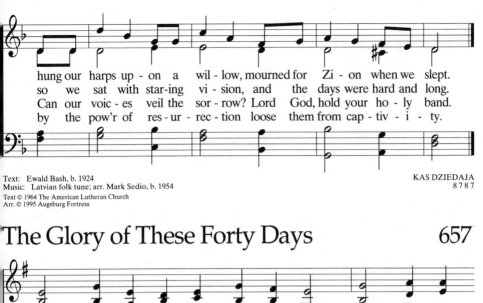

hung our harps up - on a wil - low, mourned for Zi - on when we slept.
so we sat with star-ing vi - sion, and the days were hard and long.
Can our voic - es veil the sor - row? Lord God, hold your ho - ly band.
by the pow'r of res - ur - rec - tion loose them from cap - tiv - i - ty.

Text: Ewald Bash, b. 1924
Music: Latvian folk tune; arr. Mark Sedio, b. 1954
Text © 1964 The American Lutheran Church
Arr. © 1995 Augsburg Fortress

KAS DZIEDAJA
8 7 8 7

The Glory of These Forty Days 657

1 The glo - ry of these for - ty days we cel - e -
2 A - lone and fast - ing Mo - ses saw the lov - ing
3 So Dan - iel trained his mys - tic sight, de - liv - ered
4 Then grant, O God, that we may, too, re - turn in

brate with songs of praise; for Christ, through whom all
God who gave the law; and to E - li - jah,
from the li - ons' might; and John, the Bride - groom's
fast and prayer to you. Our spir - its strength - en

things were made, him - self has fast - ed and has prayed.
fast - ing, came the steeds and char - i - ots of flame.
friend, be - came the her - ald of Mes - si - ah's name.
with your grace, and give us joy to see your face.

Text: Latin hymn, 11th cent.; tr. Maurice F. Bell, 1862–1947, alt.
Music: attr. Martin Luther, 1483–1546; *Geistliche Lieder*, 1543
Tr. © 1906 Oxford University Press, London

ERHALT UNS, HERR
L M

658 The Word of God Is Source and Seed

1 The Word of God is source and seed; it comes to
2 The Word of God is breath and life; it comes to
3 The Word of God is flesh and grace who comes to

die and sprout and grow. So make your dark earth wel-come-
heal and wake and save. So let the Spir-it touch and
sing, to laugh and cry. So dare to be as Je-sus

warm; root deep the grain God bent to sow.
mend and rouse your dry bones from their grave.
was, who came to live and love and die.

Refrain

Gau-de - a - mus Do - mi - no, gau - de - a - mus Do - mi - no,
In the Lord let us re - joice, in the Lord let us re - joice,

gau - de - a - mus Do - mi - no!
in the Lord let us re - joice!

Latin pronunciation: gaù-dĕ-à-mùs dô-mē-nō

Text: Delores Dufner, OSB, b. 1939
Music: David Hurd, b. 1950
Text © 1983, 1993 Sisters of St. Benedict, St. Joseph, MN, admin. Augsburg Fortress
Music © 1995 Augsburg Fortress

GAUDEAMUS DOMINO
L M and refrain

659

O Sun of Justice

1. O Sun of jus - tice, Je - sus Christ, dis - pel the dark - ness
2. In this our "time ac - cept - a - ble" touch ev - 'ry heart with
3. The day, your day, in beau - ty dawns when in your light earth
4. O lov - ing Trin - i - ty, our God, to you we bow through

of our hearts, till your blest light makes night - time flee
sor - row, Lord, that, turned from sin, re - newed by grace,
blooms a - new; led back a - gain to life's true way,
end - less days, and in your grace new - born we sing

and brings the joys your day im - parts.
we may press on toward love's re - ward.
may we, for - giv'n, re - joice in you.
new hymns of grat - i - tude and praise. A - men

Text: Latin hymn, 6th cent.; tr. Peter J. Scagnelli, b. 1949
Music: Plainsong, mode 1; arr. Theodore Marier, *ICEL Resource Collection*
Tr. © Peter J. Scagnelli

JESU DULCIS MEMORIA
L M

alt. tune: TALLIS' CANON

I Want Jesus to Walk with Me 660

1 I want Je - sus to walk with me;
2 In my tri - als, Lord, walk with me;
3 When I'm in trou - ble, Lord, walk with me;

I want Je - sus to walk with me;
in my tri - als, Lord, walk with me;
When I'm in trou - ble, Lord, walk with me;

all a - long my pil - grim jour - ney,
when my heart is al - most break - ing,
when my head is bowed in sor - row,

Lord, I want Je - sus to walk with me.
Lord, I want Je - sus to walk with me.
Lord, I want Je - sus to walk with me.

Text: African American spiritual
Music: African American spiritual; arr. J. Jefferson Cleveland, b. 1937, Verolga Nix, b. 1933
Arr. © 1981 Abingdon Press

SOJOURNER
irregular

661 My Song Is Love Unknown

1 My song is love un - known, my Sav - ior's love to
2 He came from his blest throne sal - va - tion to be -
3 Some - times they strew his way and his sweet prais - es
4 Why, what hath my Lord done? What makes this rage and
5 They rise and needs will have my dear Lord made a -

me, love to the love - less shown that they might love - ly
stow; but men made strange, and none the longed-for Christ would
sing; re - sound-ing all the day ho - san - nas to their
spite? He made the lame to run, he gave the blind their
way; a mur - der - er they save, the prince of life they

be. Oh, who am I that for my sake
know. But, oh, my friend, my friend in - deed,
King. Then "Cru - ci - fy!" is all their breath,
sight. Sweet in - ju - ries! Yet they at these
slay. Yet cheer - ful he to suff - 'ring goes

my Lord should take frail flesh and die?
who at my need his life did spend!
and for his death they thirst and cry.
them - selves dis - please and 'gainst him rise.
that he his foes from thence might free.

6   In life no house, no home
    my Lord on earth might have;
    in death no friendly tomb
    but what a stranger gave.
    What may I say? Heav'n was his home
    but mine the tomb wherein he lay.

7   Here might I stay and sing—
    no story so divine!
    Never was love, dear King,
    never was grief like thine.
    This is my friend, in whose sweet praise
    I all my days could gladly spend!

Text: Samuel Crossman, c. 1624–1683
Music: John Ireland, 1879–1962
Music © 1924 John Ireland, admin. The John Ireland Trust

LOVE UNKNOWN
66664444

Restore in Us, O God   662

1 Re - store in us, O God, the splen - dor of your
2 O Spir - it, wake in us the won - der of your
3 Bring us, O Christ, to share the full - ness of your
4 Three per - soned God, ful - fill the prom - ise of your

love;   re - new your im - age in our hearts,
power;   from fruit - less fear un - furl our lives
joy;   bap - tize us in the ris - en life
grace,   that we, when all our search - ing ends,

1–3

and all our sins re - move.
like spring-time bud and flower.
that death can - not de - stroy.

4

may   see you face to face.

Text: Carl P. Daw, Jr., b. 1944
Music: David Hurd, b. 1950
Text © 1989 Hope Publishing Co.
Music © 1995 Augsburg Fortress

CATECHUMEN
S M

alt. tune: POTSDAM

When Twilight Comes

Evening Song

663

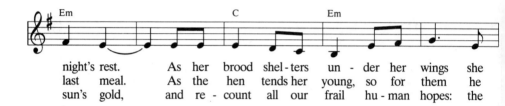

1 When twi-light comes and the sun sets, moth-er hen pre-pares for
2 One day the Rab-bi, Lord Je-sus, called the twelve to share his
3 So gath-er 'round once a-gain, friends, touched by fad-ing glow of

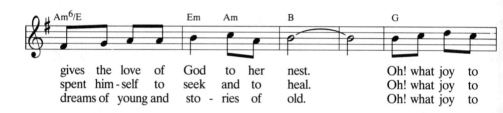

night's rest. As her brood shel-ters un-der her wings she
last meal. As the hen tends her young, so for them he
sun's gold, and re-count all our frail hu-man hopes: the

gives the love of God to her nest. Oh! what joy to
spent him-self to seek and to heal. Oh! what joy to
dreams of young and sto-ries of old. Oh! what joy to

feel her warm heart-beat and be near her all night long;
be with Christ Je-sus, hear his voice, oh! sheer de-light,
pray close to-geth-er, kneel-ing as one fam-i-ly,

so the young can find re-pose, then re-new to-mor-row's song.
and re-ceive his ser-vant care: all be-fore the com-ing night.
by a moth-er's love em-braced in the bless-ed Trin-i-ty.

Text: Moises Andrade, tr. James Minchin
Music: Francisco Feliciano, b. 1941
Tr. © James Minchin, music © Francisco Feliciano, admin. Asian Institute for Liturgy & Music

DAPIT HAPON
88999777

A New Commandment 664

Text: John 13:34–35
Music: Anonymous

NEW COMMANDMENT
irregular

Ubi Caritas et Amor
Where True Charity and Love Abide

665

U - bi ca - ri - tas et a - mor,
Where true char - i - ty and love a - bide,

u - bi ca - ri - tas De - us i - bi est.
God is dwell - ing there; God is dwell - ing there.

Text: Latin, 8th cent.
Music: Jacques Berthier, 1923–1994
Music © 1979 Les Presses de Taizé, admin. GIA Publications, Inc.

TAIZÉ UBI CARITAS
irregular

666

Great God, Your Love Has Called Us

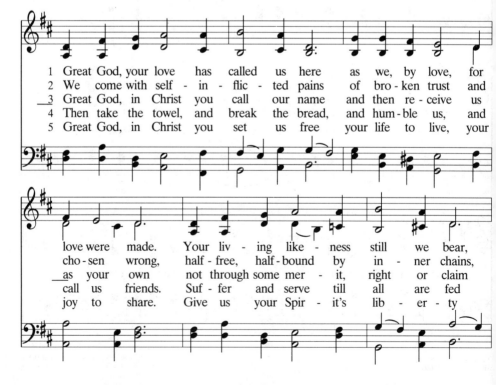

1 Great God, your love has called us here as we, by love, for
2 We come with self - in - flic - ted pains of bro - ken trust and
3 Great God, in Christ you call our name and then re - ceive us
4 Then take the towel, and break the bread, and hum - ble us, and
5 Great God, in Christ you set us free your life to live, your

love were made. Your liv - ing like - ness still we bear,
cho - sen wrong, half - free, half - bound by in - ner chains,
as your own not through some mer - it, right or claim
call us friends. Suf - fer and serve till all are fed
joy to share. Give us your Spir - it's lib - er - ty

though marred, dis - hon - ored, dis - o - beyed. We come, with all our
by so - cial forc - es swept a - long, by powers and sys - tems
but by your gra - cious love a - lone. We strain to glimpse your
and show how grand - ly love in - tends to work till all cre -
to turn from guilt and dull de - spair, and of - fer all that

heart and mind your call to hear, your love to find.
close con - fined yet seek - ing hope for hu - man - kind.
mer - cy seat and find you kneel - ing at our feet.
a - tion sings, to fill all worlds, to crown all things.
faith can do while love is mak - ing all things new.

Text: Brian Wren, b. 1936
Music: Norman Cocker, 1889–1953

Text © 1977 Hope Publishing Co.
Music © Oxford University Press, London

RYBURN
888888

alt. tune: ST. CATHERINE

Stay Here

667

Stay here and keep watch with me. The hour has come.

Stay here and keep watch with me. Watch and pray.

Text: Matt. 26:38,45; Taizé Community
Music: Jacques Berthier, 1923–1994

© 1984 Les Presses de Taizé, admin. GIA Publications, Inc.

STAY HERE
irregular

668

There in God's Garden

1 There in God's gar - den stands the Tree of Wis - dom,
2 Its name is Je - sus, name that says, "Our Sa - vior!"
3 Thorns not its own are tan - gled in its fo - liage;
4 See how its branch - es reach to us in wel - come;

whose leaves hold forth the heal - ing of the na - tions:
There on its branch - es see the scars of suf - f'ring;
our greed has starved it, our de - spite has choked it.
hear what the Voice says, "Come to me, ye wea - ry!

Tree of all knowl - edge, Tree of all com -
see where the ten - drils of our hu - man
Yet, look! it lives! its grief has not de -
Give me your sick - ness, give me all your

pas - sion, Tree of all beau - ty.
self - hood feed on its life - blood.
stroyed it nor fire con - sumed it.
sor - row, I will give bless - ing."

5 This is my ending,
   this my resurrection;
  into your hands, Lord,
   I commit my spirit.
  This have I searched for;
   now I can possess it.
    This ground is holy.

6 All heav'n is singing,
  "Thanks to Christ whose Passion
  offers in mercy
   healing, strength, and pardon.
  Peoples and nations,
   take it, take it freely!"
    Amen! My Master!

Text: Király Imre von Pécselyi, c. 1590–c. 1641; tr. Erik Routley, 1917–1982
Music: K. Lee Scott, b. 1950
Tr. © 1976 Hinshaw Music, Inc.
Music © 1987 MorningStar Music Publishers

SHADES MOUNTAIN
11 11 11 5

alt. tune: HERZLIEBSTER JESU

Come Away to the Skies   669

1 Come a - way to the skies, my be - lov - ed, a - rise and re-
2 For thy glo - ry we were first cre - at - ed to share both the
3 We with thanks do ap - prove the de - sign of that love which has
4 Hal - le - lu - jah we sing to our Fa - ther and King, and our

joice in the day you were born: on this fes - ti - val day,
na - ture and king - dom di - vine; now cre - at - ed a - gain,
joined us to Je - sus'. . . name; so u - nit - ed in heart,
rap - tur - ous prais - es re - peat: to the Lamb that was slain,

come ex - ult - ing a - way, and with sing - ing to Zi - on re - turn.
that our lives may re - main through - out time and e - ter - ni - ty thine.
let us nev - er - more part, till we meet at the feast of the Lamb.
hal - le - lu - jah a - gain; sing, all heav - en, and fall at his feet.

Text: Charles Wesley, 1707–1788
Music: *A Supplement to the Kentucky Harmony,* c. 1821; arr. David Cherwien, b. 1957
Arr. © 1995 Augsburg Fortress

MIDDLEBURY
669669

670 When Israel Was in Egypt's Land

1 When Is-rael was in E - gypt's land,
2 The Lord told Mo - ses what to do,
3 The pillar of cloud shall clear the way,
4 As Is-rael stood by the wa - ter - side, let my peo-ple go;
5 When they had reached the oth - er shore,
6 Oh, let us all from bond-age flee,

op - pressed so hard they could not stand,
to lead the childr'n of Is - rael through,
a fire by night, a shade by day,
at God's com-mand it did di - vide, let my peo-ple go.
they sang the song of tri - umph o'er,
and let us all in Christ be free,

Refrain

Go down, Mo - ses, way down in E - gypt's land,

tell old Pha - raoh: let my peo-ple go.

Text: African American spiritual
Music: African American spiritual; arr. John R. Work, 1871–1925

TUBMAN
8 5 8 5 and refrain

Alleluia, Alleluia, Give Thanks 671

Refrain F | Dm | Gm | C

Al - le - lu - ia, al - le - lu - ia, give thanks to the ris - en Lord;

F | Dm | Gm | C | F

al - le - lu - ia, al - le - lu - ia, give praise to his name.

F | Dm | B♭ | C

1 Je - sus is Lord of all the earth;
2 Spread the good news o'er all the earth:
3 We have been cru - ci - fied with Christ;
4 God has pro - claimed the just re - ward:
5 Come, let us praise the liv - ing God,

F | Dm | B♭ | C *Refrain*

he is the king of cre - a - tion.
Je - sus has died and has ris - en.
now we shall live . . . for - ev - er.
life for all peo - ple, al - le - lu - ia.
joy - ful - ly sing to our Sav - ior.

Text: Donald Fishel, b. 1950
Music: Donald Fishel, b. 1950; arr. Betty Pulkingham, b. 1928
© 1973 Word of God Music, admin. The Copyright Co.

ALLELUIA NO. 1
8 8 and refrain

672 Christ Is Risen! Shout Hosanna!

1 Christ is ris - en! Shout ho - san - na! Cel - e - brate this day of
2 Christ is ris - en! Raise your spir - its from the cav - erns of de -
3 Christ is ris - en! Earth and heav - en nev - er - more shall be the

days! Christ is ris - en! Hush in won - der:
spair. Walk with glad - ness in the morn - ing
same. Break the bread of new cre - a - tion

all cre - a - tion is a - mazed. In the des - ert all - sur -
See what love can do and dare. Drink the wine of res - ur -
where the world is still in pain. Tell its grim, de - mon - ic

round - ing, see, a spread - ing tree has grown.
rec - tion. Not a ser - vant, but a friend,
chor - us: "Christ is ris - en! Get you gone!"

Heal-ing leaves of grace a-bound-ing bring a taste of love un-known.
Je - sus is our strong com-pan - ion. Joy and peace shall nev - er end.
God the first and last is with us. Sing ho-san - na, ev - 'ry - one!

Text: Brian Wren, b. 1936
Music: William P. Rowan, b. 1951
© 1986 Hope Publishing Co.

JACKSON NEW
8 7 8 7 D

alt. tune: AUSTRIA

I'm So Glad Jesus Lifted Me 673

1 I'm so glad, Je-sus lift-ed me. I'm so glad,
2 Satan had me bound, Satan had me bound,
3 When I was in trouble, When I was in trouble,

Je-sus lift-ed me. I'm so glad,
Satan had me bound,
When I was in trouble,

Je-sus lift-ed me,

sing-ing glo-ry, hal-le-lu-jah! Je-sus lift-ed me.

Text: African American spiritual
Music: African American spiritual; arr. *With One Voice*, 1995
Arr. © 1995 Augsburg Fortress

JESUS LIFTED ME
irregular

674 Alleluia! Jesus Is Risen

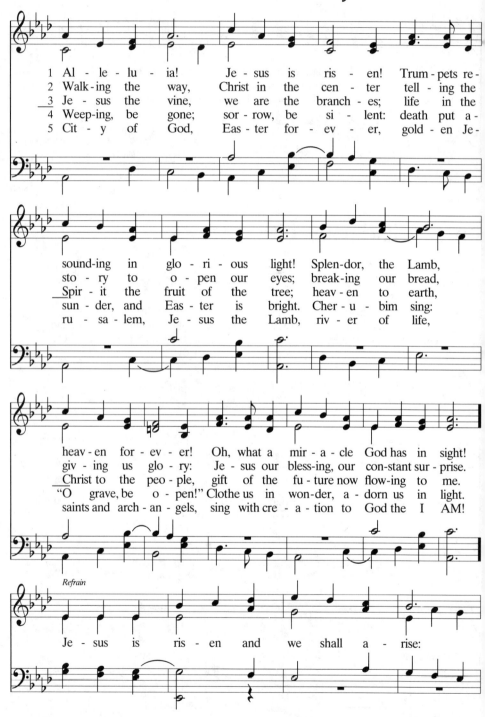

1 Al - le - lu - ia! Je - sus is ris - en! Trum - pets re-
2 Walk - ing the way, Christ in the cen - ter tell - ing the
3 Je - sus the vine, we are the branch - es; life in the
4 Weep - ing, be gone; sor - row, be si - lent: death put a-
5 Cit - y of God, Eas - ter for - ev - er, gold - en Je-

sound - ing in glo - ri - ous light! Splen - dor, the Lamb,
sto - ry to o - pen our eyes; break - ing our bread,
Spir - it the fruit of the tree; heav - en to earth,
sun - der, and Eas - ter is bright. Cher - u - bim sing:
ru - sa - lem, Je - sus the Lamb, riv - er of life,

heav - en for - ev - er! Oh, what a mir - a - cle God has in sight!
giv - ing us glo - ry: Je - sus our bless - ing, our con - stant sur - prise.
Christ to the peo - ple, gift of the fu - ture now flow - ing to me.
"O grave, be o - pen!" Clothe us in won - der, a - dorn us in light.
saints and arch - an - gels, sing with cre - a - tion to God the I AM!

Refrain

Je - sus is ris - en and we shall a - rise:

Give God the glo - ry! Al - le - lu - ia!

Text: Herbert F. Brokering, b. 1926
Music: David N. Johnson, 1922–1987
Text © 1995 Augsburg Fortress
Music © 1969 Contemporary Worship 1, admin. Augsburg Fortress

EARTH AND ALL STARS
4 5 10 4 5 10 and refrain

We Walk by Faith and Not by Sight 675

1 We walk by faith and not by sight; with
2 We may not touch your hands and side, nor
3 Help then, O Lord, our un - be - lief; and
4 That, when our life of faith is done, in

gra - cious words draw near, O Christ, who spoke as
fol - low where you trod; but in your prom - ise
may our faith a - bound to call on you when
realms of clear - er light we may be - hold you

none e'er spoke: "My peace be with you here."
we re - joice, and cry, "My Lord and God!"
you are near and seek where you are found:
as you are, with full and end - less sight.

Text: Henry Alford, 1810–1871, alt.
Music: Samuel McFarland, fl. 1816; arr. With One Voice, 1995
Arr. © 1995 Augsburg Fortress

DUNLAP'S CREEK
C M

alternate tune: NEW BRITAIN

676

This Joyful Eastertide

1 This joy - ful Eas - ter - tide, a - way with sin and
2 My flesh in hope shall rest and for a sea - son
3 Death's flood has lost its chill since Je - sus crossed the

sor - row! My love, the Cru - ci - fied, has
slum - ber till trump from east to west shall
riv - er; Lov - er of souls, from ill my

sprung to life this mor - row.
wake the dead in num - ber.
pass - ing soul de - liv - er.

Refrain

Had Christ, who once was

slain, not burst his three-day pris - on, our faith had been in vain.

But now has Christ a - ris - en, a - ris - en, a -

ris - en, a - ris - - - en.

Text: George Woodward, 1848–1934
Music: Dutch folk tune, 17th cent., arr. Charles Wood, 1866–1926

VRUECHTEN
6 7 6 7 and refrain

Alleluia Canon

677

1
Al - le - lu - ia, al - le - lu - ia, al - le - lu - ia, al - le - lu - ia.

2
Al - le - lu - ia, al - le - lu - ia, al - le - lu - ia, al - le - lu - ia.

3
Al - le - lu - ia, al - le - lu - ia.

Music: W.A. Mozart, 1756–1791; from *Exultate, Jubilate,* adapt.

MOZART ALLELUIA
irregular

678

Christ Has Arisen, Alleluia

1 Christ has a - ris - en, al - le - lu - ia.
2 For three long days the grave did its worst
3 The an - gel said to them, "Do not fear.
4 "Go spread the news: he's not in the grave.
5 Christ has a - ris - en to set us free.

Re - joice and praise him, al - le - lu - ia.
un - til its strength by God was dis - persed.
You look for Je - sus who is not here.
He has a - ris - en this world to save.
Al - le - lu - ia, to him prais - es be.

For our re - deem - er burst from the tomb,
He who gives life did death un - der - go,
See for your - selves the tomb is all bare.
Je - sus' re - deem - ing la - bors are done.
Je - sus is liv - ing! Let us all sing;

e - ven from death, dis - pel - ling its gloom.
and in its con - quest his might did show.
On - ly the grave cloths are ly - ing there."
E - ven the bat - tle with sin is won."
he reigns tri - um - phant, heav - en - ly king.

Text: Bernard Kyamanywa, b. 1938, tr. Howard S. Olson, b. 1922
Music: Traditional Tanzanian
Tr. © 1977 Augsburg Fortress

MFURAHINI, HALELUYA
9 9 9 9 and refrain

679 Our Paschal Lamb, That Sets Us Free

1 Our Pas - chal Lamb, that
2 Let all our lives now
3 Let all our deeds, u -

sets us free, is sac - ri - ficed. Oh, keep the feast of free - dom
cel - e - brate the feast; let mal - ice die. Let love grow strong a -
na - ni - mous con - fess him as our Lord who by the Spir - it

gal - lant - ly; let al - le - lu - ias leap:
new and great, let truth stamp out the lie.
lives in us, the Fa - ther's liv - ing Word.

Refrain

Al - le - lu - ia, al - le - lu - ia. Sing al - le - lu - ia, cry a - loud:

1 Al - le - lu - ia! A - men!

2 Al - le - lu - ia! A - men!

Text: Martin H. Franzmann, 1907–1976
Music: Richard Proulx, b. 1937
Text © 1974, music © 1995 Augsburg Fortress

MANNION
C M and refrain

680

O Spirit of Life

1 O Spir - it of life, O Spir - it of God,
2 O Spir - it of life, O Spir - it of God,
3 O Spir - it of life, O Spir - it of God,
4 O Spir - it of life, O Spir - it of God,

in ev - 'ry need you bring us aid,
in - crease our faith in our dear Lord;
make us to love your sa - cred Word;
en - light - en us by that same Word;

pro - ceed - ing forth from God's great throne,
un - less your grace the power should give,
the ho - ly flame of love im - part,
teach us to know God's ra - diant love,

from God, the Fa - ther and the Son;
none can be - lieve in Christ and live;
that char - i - ty may warm each heart;
lead us to Christ who reigns a - bove;

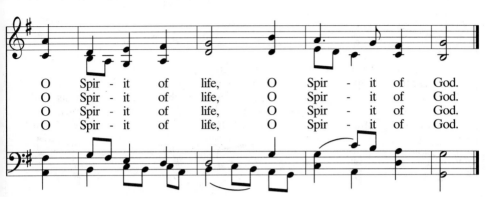

O Spir - it of life, O Spir - it of God.
O Spir - it of life, O Spir - it of God.
O Spir - it of life, O Spir - it of God.
O Spir - it of life, O Spir - it of God.

Text: Johann Niedling, 1602–1668; tr. John C. Mattes, 1876–1948
Music: *Geistliche Kirchengesäng*, 1623; arr. J.S. Bach, 1685–1750

O HEILIGER GEIST
10 8 8 8 10

Come, O Holy Spirit, Come
Wa wa wa Emimimo

681

Come, O Ho - ly Spir - it, come,
Wa wa wa E - mi - mi - mo,

Ho - ly Spir - it, come.
E - mi - o - lo - ye.

Come, al - might - y Spir - it, come,
Wa wa wa A - lag - ba - ra,

al - might - y Spir - it, come.
A - lag - ba - ra - me - ta.

Come, come, come.
Wa - o wa - o wa - o.

O Spir - it, come.
E - mi - mi - mo.

Text: Nigerian traditional, tr. I-to Loh, b. 1936
Music: Taught by Samuel Solanke; arr. I-to Loh, b. 1936
Tr. and music © 1986 World Council of Churches

WA EMIMIMO
irregular

682 Praise the Spirit in Creation

1 Praise the Spir - it in cre - a - tion, breath of
2 Praise the Spir - it, close com - pan - ion of our
3 Praise the Spir - it, who en - light - ened priests and
4 Tell of how the as - cend - ed Je - sus armed a
5 Pray we then, O Lord the Spir - it, on our

God, life's or - i - gin: Spir - it, mov - ing on the
in - most thoughts and ways: who, in show - ing us God's
proph - ets with the Word; ho - ly truth be - hind the
peo - ple for his own; how a hun - dred men and
lives de - scend in might; let your flame break out with -

wa - ters, quick-'ning worlds to life with - in, source of
won - ders, is for us the pow'r to gaze; and God's
wis - doms which as yet know not our Lord; by whose
wom - en turned the known world up - side down, to its
in us, fire our hearts and clear our sight, till, white -

breath to all things breath-ing, life in whom all lives be - gin.
will, to those who lis - ten, by a still small voice con - veys.
love and pow'r, in Je - sus, God by us was seen and heard.
dark and fur - thest cor - ners by the wind of heav - en blown.
hot in your pos - ses - sion, we, too, set the world a - light.

Text: Michael Hewlett, b. 1916, alt.
Music: David Hurd, b. 1950
Text © Oxford University Press, *English Praise*, 1975
Music © 1983 GIA Publications, Inc.

JULION
878787

alt. tune: PRAISE, MY SOUL

Loving Spirit

683

1 Lov - ing Spir - it, lov - ing Spir - it, you have cho - sen me to be—
2 Like a moth-er you en - fold me, hold my life with - in your own,
3 Like a fa - ther you pro - tect me, teach me the dis - cern-ing eye,
4 Friend and lov - er, in your close-ness I am known and held and blessed:
5 Lov - ing Spir - it, lov - ing Spir - it, you have cho - sen me to be—

you have drawn me to your won - der, you have set your sign on me.
feed me with your ver - y bod - y, form me of your flesh and bone.
hoist me up up - on your shoul-der, let me see the world from high.
in your prom - ise is my com - fort, in your pres-ence I may rest.
you have drawn me to your won - der, you have set your sign on me.

Text: Shirley Erena Murray, b. 1931
Music: Rusty Edwards, b. 1955
Text © 1987 The Hymn Society, admin. Hope Publishing Co.
Music © 1993 Hope Publishing Co.

BETH
8787

alt. tune: OMNI DIE

684 Spirit, Spirit of Gentleness

Refrain

Spir - it, Spir-it of gen - tle-ness, blow through the wil - der-ness

call-ing and free; Spir - it, Spir-it of rest-less-ness,

stir me from plac - id-ness, wind, wind on the sea.

1 You moved on the wa - ters, you called to the deep,
2 You swept through the des - ert, you stung with the sand
3 You sang in a sta - ble, you cried from a hill,
4 You call from to - mor - row, you break an - cient schemes.

then you coaxed up the moun - tains from the val - leys of sleep;
and you goad - ed your peo - ple with a law and a land;
then you whis - pered in si - lence when the whole world was still;
From the bond - age of sor - row all the cap - tives dream dreams;

and o - ver the e - ons you called to each thing:
and when they were blind - ed with i - dols and lies,
and down in the cit - y you called once a - gain,
our wom - en see vi - sions, our men clear their eyes.

"A - wake from your slum - bers and rise on your wings."
then you spoke through your proph - ets to o - pen their eyes.
when you blew through your peo - ple on the rush of the wind.
With . . . bold new de - ci - sions your peo-ple a - rise.

Refrain

Text: James K. Manley, b. 1940
Music: James K. Manley, b. 1940
© 1978 James K. Manley

SPIRIT
irregular

685 Like the Murmur of the Dove's Song

1 Like the mur - mur of the dove's song, like the chal - lenge of her
2 To the mem - bers of Christ's bod - y, to the branch-es of the
3 With the heal - ing of di - vi - sion, with the cease-less voice of

flight, like the vig - or of the wind's rush, like the
vine, to the Church in faith as - sem - bled, to our
prayer, with the power to love and wit - ness, with the

new flame's ea - ger might: come, Ho - ly Spir - it, come.
midst as gift and sign: come, Ho - ly Spir - it, come.
peace be - yond com - pare: come, Ho - ly Spir - it, come.

Text: Carl P. Daw, Jr., b. 1944
Music: Peter Cutts, b. 1937
Text © 1982, music © 1989 Hope Publishing Co.

BRIDEGROOM
87876

Veni Sancte Spiritus
Holy Spirit, Come to Us

686

After the ostinato has begun, verses may be sung over it;
space is left between the verses as the ostinato continues.

1 Come, Ho - ly Spir - it, from heav - en shine forth

with your glo - rious light. Ve - ni San - cte Spi - ri - tus.

2 Come from the four winds, O Spir - it, come, Breath of

God; dis - perse the shad - ows o - ver us, re -

new and strength-en your peo - ple. Ve - ni San - cte Spi - ri - tus.

Latin pronunciation: vĕ-nē sàn-ktĕ spē-rē-tùs

Text: Pentecost Sequence; Taizé Community, 1978
Music: Jacques Berthier, 1923–1994
© 1979 Les Presses de Taizé, admin. GIA Publications, Inc.

TAIZÉ VENI SANCTE
irregular

687 Gracious Spirit, Heed Our Pleading

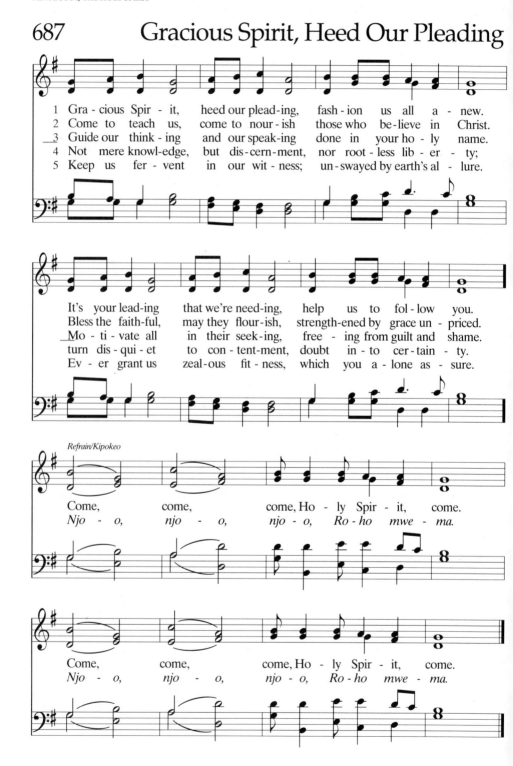

1 Gra - cious Spir - it, heed our plead-ing, fash - ion us all a - new.
2 Come to teach us, come to nour - ish those who be-lieve in Christ.
3 Guide our think - ing and our speak-ing done in your ho - ly name.
4 Not mere knowl-edge, but dis-cern-ment, nor root - less lib - er - ty;
5 Keep us fer - vent in our wit - ness; un-swayed by earth's al - lure.

It's your lead-ing that we're need-ing, help us to fol - low you.
Bless the faith-ful, may they flour-ish, strength-ened by grace un - priced.
Mo - ti - vate all in their seek-ing, free - ing from guilt and shame.
turn dis - qui - et to con - tent-ment, doubt in - to cer - tain - ty.
Ev - er grant us zeal-ous fit - ness, which you a - lone as - sure.

Refrain/Kipokeo

Come, come, come, Ho - ly Spir - it, come.
Njo - o, njo - o, njo - o, Ro - ho mwe - ma.

Come, come, come, Ho - ly Spir - it, come.
Njo - o, njo - o, njo - o, Ro - ho mwe - ma.

1 *Njoo kwetu, Roho mwema, Mfariji wetu.*
  Tufundishe ya mbinguni, tuwe watu wapya.   Kipokeo

2 *Utufanye waamini wa Yesu Mwokozi.*
  Tukaishi kikundini, kanisani mwako.   Kipokeo

3 *Kwa huruma tubariki, tuishi na wewe.*
  Tukatende kila kitu kuongozwa nawe.   Kipokeo

4 *Roho mwema, Mfariji, utupe hekima;*
  Tukiwaza na kutenda, yote yawe yako.   Kipokeo

5 *Tudumishe tuwe hai na ukweli wako.*
  Tusivutwe na dunia, tushu'die neema.   Kipokeo

Text: Wilson Niwagila; tr. Howard S. Olson, b. 1922
Music: Wilson Niwagila; arr. Egil Hovland, b. 1924
Swahili and English texts and tune © Lutheran Theological College, Makumira, Tanzania, arr. © Egil Hovland

NJOO KWETU, ROHO MWEMA
C M and refrain

O Holy Spirit, Root of Life   688

1 O Ho - ly Spir - it, root of life, cre - a - tor,
2 E - ter - nal Vig - or, Sav - ing One, you free us
3 O ho - ly Wis - dom, soar - ing power, en - com - pass

cleans - er of all things: a - noint our wounds, a -
by your liv - ing Word, be - com - ing flesh to
us with wings un - furled, and car - ry us, en -

wak - en us with lus - trous move - ment of your wings.
wear our pain, and all cre - a - tion is re - stored.
cir - cling all a - bove, be - low, and through the world.

Text: Jean Janzen, b. 1933, based on Hildegard of Bingen, 1078–1179
Music: European tune, 15th cent., adapt. Michael Praetorius, 1571–1621
Text © 1991 Jean Janzen

PUER NOBIS
L M

689 Rejoice in God's Saints

1 Re - joice in God's saints to - day and all days!
2 Some march with e - vents to turn them God's way;
3 Re - joice in those saints, un - praised and un - known,
4 Re - joice in God's saints to - day and all days!

A world with - out saints for - gets how to praise.
some need to with - draw, the bet - ter to pray;
who bear some - one's cross, or shoul - der their own:
A world with - out saints for - gets how to praise.

Their faith in ac - quir - ing the hab - it of prayer,
some car - ry the Gos - pel through fire and through flood;
they share our com - plain - ing, our com - forts, our cares:
In lov - ing, in liv - ing, they prove it is true:

their depth of a - dor - ing, Lord, help us to share.
our world is their par - ish, their pur - pose is God.
what pa - tience in car - ing, what cour - age is theirs!
their way of self - giv - ing, Lord, leads us to you.

Text: Fred Pratt Green, b. 1903
Music: C. Hubert H. Parry, 1848–1918
Text © 1973 Hope Publishing Co.

LAUDATE DOMINUM
10 10 11 11

alt. tune: LYONS

Shall We Gather at the River 690

1 Shall we gath-er at the riv - er, where bright an-gel feet have trod,
2 On the mar-gin of the riv - er, wash - ing up its sil - ver spray,
3 Ere we reach the shin-ing riv - er, lay we ev-'ry bur-den down;
4 Soon we'll reach the shin-ing riv - er, soon our pil-grim-age will cease;

with its crys-tal tide for-ev - er flow-ing by the throne of God?
we will walk and wor-ship ev - er, all the hap-py gold-en day.
grace our spir-its will de-liv - er, and pro-vide a robe and crown.
soon our hap-py hearts will quiv - er with the mel-o-dy of peace.

Refrain

Yes, we'll gath-er at the riv - er, the beau-ti-ful, the beau-ti-ful riv - er;

gath-er with the saints at the riv - er that flows by the throne of God.

Text: Robert Lowry, 1826–1899
Music: Robert Lowry, 1826–1899

HANSON PLACE
8 7 8 7 and refrain

691 Sing with All the Saints in Glory

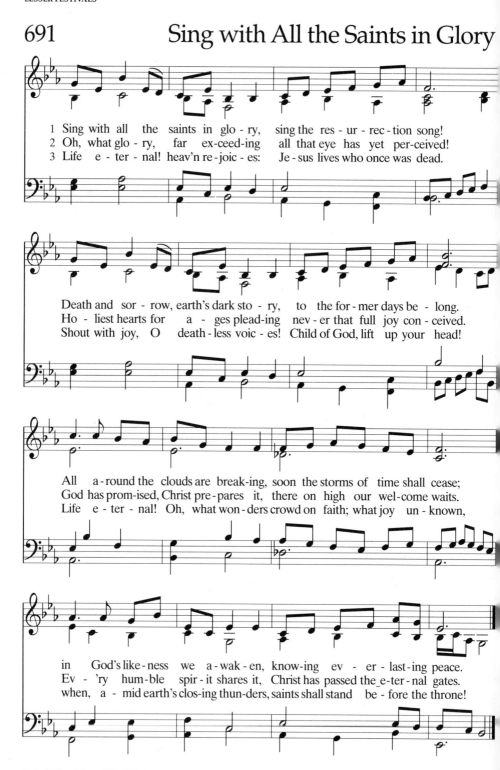

1 Sing with all the saints in glo - ry, sing the res - ur - rec - tion song!
2 Oh, what glo - ry, far ex-ceed-ing all that eye has yet per-ceived!
3 Life e - ter - nal! heav'n re - joic - es: Je - sus lives who once was dead.

Death and sor - row, earth's dark sto - ry, to the for - mer days be - long.
Ho - liest hearts for a - ges plead-ing nev - er that full joy con - ceived.
Shout with joy, O death-less voic - es! Child of God, lift up your head!

All a-round the clouds are break-ing, soon the storms of time shall cease;
God has prom-ised, Christ pre-pares it, there on high our wel-come waits.
Life e - ter - nal! Oh, what won-ders crowd on faith; what joy un - known,

in God's like-ness we a-wak-en, know-ing ev - er - last-ing peace.
Ev - 'ry hum-ble spir-it shares it, Christ has passed the e-ter-nal gates.
when, a - mid earth's clos-ing thun-ders, saints shall stand be - fore the throne!

Text: William J. Irons, 1812–1883, alt.
Music: William B. Roberts, b. 1947
Music © 1995 Augsburg Fortress

MISSISSIPPI
8 7 8 7 D

alt. tune: HYMN TO JOY

For All the Faithful Women

692

1 For all the faith-ful wom-en who served in days of old,
2 We praise your name for Mir-iam who sang tri - um-phant-ly
3 To Han - nah, pray-ing child-less be-fore the throne of grace,
4 We sing of Mar - y, moth-er, fair maid - en, full of grace.
5 We praise the oth-er Mar - y who came at Eas-ter dawn

to you shall thanks be giv-en; to all, their sto - ry told.
while Phar - aoh's vaunt-ed ar - my lay drowned be - neath the sea.
you gave a son whose ser - vice would be be - fore your face.
She bore the Christ, our broth-er, who came to save our race.
and near the tomb did tar - ry, but found her Lord was gone.

They served with strength and glad-ness in tasks your wis-dom gave.
As Is - rael marched to free-dom, her chains of bond-age gone,
Grant us her per - se - ver-ance; Lord, teach us how to pray,
May we, with her, sur - ren - der our-selves to your com-mand
As joy - ful - ly she saw him in res - ur - rec-tion light,

To you their lives bore wit - ness, pro-claimed your pow'r to save.
so may we reach the king-dom your might - y arm has won.
to trust in your de - liv - 'rance when dark - ness hides our way.
and lay up - on your al - tar our gifts of heart and hand.
may we by faith be-hold him, the day who ends all night.

Text: Herman G. Stuempfle, Jr. b. 1923
Music: Doreen Potter, 1925–1980
Text © 1993 GIA Publications, Inc.
Music © 1975 Hope Publishing Co.

BARONITA
7 6 7 6 D

alt. tune: AURELIA

693 Baptized in Water

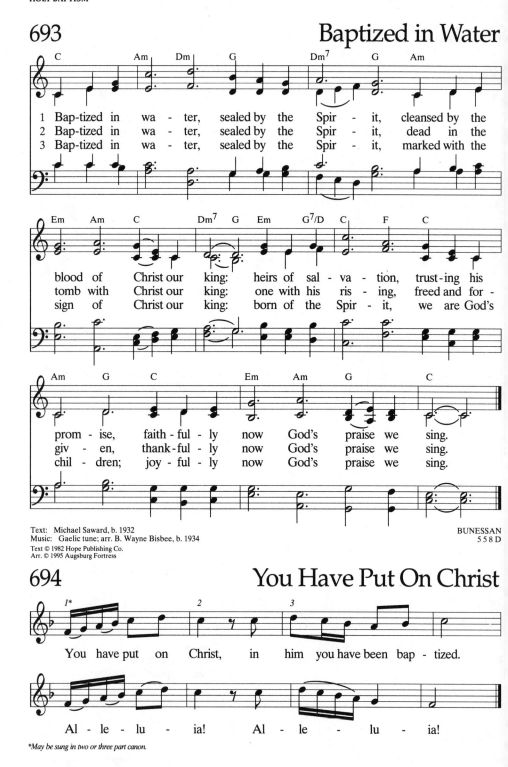

1 Bap-tized in wa - ter, sealed by the Spir - it, cleansed by the blood of Christ our king: heirs of sal - va - tion, trust-ing his prom - ise, faith-ful - ly now God's praise we sing.

2 Bap-tized in wa - ter, sealed by the Spir - it, dead in the tomb with Christ our king: one with his ris - ing, freed and for - giv - en, thank-ful - ly now God's praise we sing.

3 Bap-tized in wa - ter, sealed by the Spir - it, marked with the sign of Christ our king: born of the Spir - it, we are God's chil - dren; joy-ful - ly now God's praise we sing.

Text: Michael Saward, b. 1932
Music: Gaelic tune; arr. B. Wayne Bisbee, b. 1934
Text © 1982 Hope Publishing Co.
Arr. © 1995 Augsburg Fortress

BUNESSAN
5 5 8 D

694 You Have Put On Christ

You have put on Christ, in him you have been bap - tized.

Al - le - lu - ia! Al - le - lu - ia!

*May be sung in two or three part canon.

Text: Gal 3:27, International Commission on English in the Liturgy
Music: Howard Hughes, b. 1930
Text © 1969, music © 1977 ICEL

BAPTIZED IN CHRIST
irregular

O Blessed Spring

695

1 O bless-ed spring, where Word and sign em - brace us
2 Through sum-mer heat of youth - ful years, un - cer - tain
3 When au - tumn cools and youth is cold, when limbs their
4 As win - ter comes, as win - ters must, we breathe our
5 Christ, ho - ly Vine, Christ, liv - ing Tree, be praised for

in - to Christ the Vine: here Christ en - joins each one to
faith, re - bel - lious tears, sus - tained by Christ's in - fus - ing
heav-y har - vest hold, then through us, warm, the Christ will
last, re - turn to dust; still held in Christ, our souls take
this blest mys - ter - y: that Word and wa - ter thus re -

be a branch of this life - giv - ing Tree.
rain, the boughs will shout for joy a - gain.
move with gifts of beau - ty, wis - dom, love.
wing and trust the prom - ise of the spring.
vive and join us to your Tree of Life.

Text: Susan Palo Cherwien, b. 1953
Music: Robert Buckley Farlee, b. 1950
Text © 1993 Susan Palo Cherwien
Music © 1993 Robert Buckley Farlee

BERGLUND
L M

alt. tune: O WALY WALY

696   I've Just Come from the Fountain

Refrain

I've just come from the foun-tain, I've just come from the foun-tain, Lord, I've just come from the foun - tain, his name's so sweet. O Lord, I've sweet.

1 O broth-er, do you love Je - sus? Yes, yes, I do love my Je - sus.
2 O sis - ter, do you love Je - sus? Yes, yes, I do love my Je - sus.
3 O sin - ner, do you love Je - sus? Yes, yes, I do love my Je - sus.

Refrain

Broth-er, do you love Je - sus? His name's so sweet. O Lord, I've
Sis - ter, do you love Je - sus? His name's so sweet. O Lord, I've
Sin - ner, do you love Je - sus? His name's so sweet. O Lord, I've

Text: African American spiritual
Music: African American spiritual; arr. James Capers, b. 1948
Arr. © 1995 Augsburg Fortress

HIS NAME SO SWEET
8 8 7 4 and refrain

Wash, O God, Our Sons and Daughters 697

1 Wash, O God, our sons and daugh-ters, where your cleans-ing wa-ters flow.
2 We who bring them long for nur - ture; by your milk may we be fed.
3 Oh, how deep your ho - ly wis - dom! Un - im - ag - ined, all your ways!

Num - ber them a - mong your peo-ple; bless as Christ blessed long a - go.
Let us join your feast, par - tak-ing cup of bless - ing, liv - ing bread.
To your name be glo - ry, hon-or! With our lives we wor-ship, praise!

Weave them gar - ments bright and spark - ling; com-pass them with love and light.
God, re - new us, guide our foot - steps; free from sin and all its snares,
We your peo - ple stand be - fore you, wa - ter-washed and Spir - it-born.

Fill, a - noint them; send your Spir-it, ho - ly dove and heart's de - light.
one with Christ in liv - ing, dy - ing, by your Spir - it, chil - dren, heirs.
By your grace, our lives we of - fer. Re-cre - ate us; God, trans-form!

Text: Ruth Duck, b. 1947
Music: *The Sacred Harp*, Philadelphia, 1844; arr. *Lutheran Book of Worship*, 1978
Text © 1989 The United Methodist Publishing House
Arr © 1978 *Lutheran Book of Worship*

BEACH SPRING
8 7 8 7 D

698 We Were Baptized in Christ Jesus

1 We were bap-tized in Christ Je - sus, we were bap - tized in his death;
2 In the wa - ter and the wit - ness, in the break-ing of the bread,
3 Glo-ry be to God the Fa - ther, glo-ry be to Christ the Son,

that as Christ was raised vic - to - rious, we might live a brand new life.
in the wait - ing arms of Je - sus who is ris - en from the dead,
glo-ry to the Ho - ly Spir - it, ev - er three and ev - er one;

And if we have been u - nit - ed in a dread-ful death like his,
God has made a new be - gin - ning from the ash - es of our past;
as it was in the be - gin - ning, glo - ry now re-sounds a - gain

we will all be re - u - nit - ed, for he lives.
in the los - ing and the win - ning we hold fast.
in a song that has no end - ing. A - men

Text: John Ylvisaker, b. 1937, alt.
Music: John Ylvisaker, b. 1937
© John Ylvisaker

OUIMETTE
87878711

Blessed Assurance

699

1 Bless-ed as - sur-ance, Je - sus is mine! Oh, what a fore-taste of glo - ry di - vine!
2 Per - fect sub-mis-sion, per-fect de-light, vi - sions of rap - ture now burst on my sight;
3 Per - fect sub-mis-sion, all is at rest; I in my Sa - vior am hap - py and blest,

Heir of sal - va - tion, pur - chase of God, born of his Spir - it, washed in his blood.
an - gels de-scend-ing bring from a-bove e - choes of mer - cy, whis - pers of love.
watch-ing and wait - ing, look - ing a-bove, filled with his good-ness, lost in his love.

Refrain

This is my sto - ry, this is my song, prais-ing my Sa - vior all the day long:

this is my sto - ry, this is my song, prais-ing my Sa - vior all the day long.

Text: Fanny J. Crosby, 1820–1915
Music: Phoebe P. Knapp, 1830–1908

ASSURANCE
9 10 9 9 and refrain

700

I Received the Living God

Refrain

I re - ceived the liv - ing God, and my heart is full of joy.

I re - ceived the liv - ing God, and my heart is full of joy.

1 Je - sus said: I am the bread knead - ed long to give you life;
2 Je - sus said: I am the way, and my Fa - ther longs for you;
3 Je - sus said: I am the truth; if you fol - low close to me,
4 Je - sus said: I am the life far from whom no thing can grow,

Refrain

you who will par - take of me need not ev - er fear to die.
so I come to bring you home to be one with us a - new.
you will know me in your heart, and my word shall make you free.
but re - ceive this liv - ing bread, and my Spir - it you shall know.

Text: Anonymous
Music: Anonymous; arr. David Cherwien, b. 1957
Arr. © 1995 Augsburg Fortress

LIVING GOD
7 7 7 7 and refrain

What Feast of Love

701

1 What feast of love is of - fered here, what ban - quet come from heav - en?
2 What light of truth is of - fered here, what cov - e - nant from heav - en?
3 What wine of love is of - fered here, what ho - ly drink from heav - en?

What food of ev - er - last - ing life, what gra - cious gift is giv - en?
What hope of ev - er - last - ing life, what won - drous word is giv - en?
What stream of ev - er - last - ing life, what pre - cious blood is giv - en?

This, this is Christ the king, the bread come down from heav - en.
This, this is Christ the king, the sun come down from heav - en.
This, this is Christ the king, the sweet - est wine of heav - en.

Oh, taste and see and sing! How sweet the man - na giv - en!
Oh, see and hear and sing! The Word of God is giv - en!
Oh, taste and see and sing! The Son of God is giv - en!

Text: Delores Dufner, OSB, b. 1939
Music: English ballad, 16th cent.
Text © 1993 Delores Dufner, OSB, admin. OCP Publications

GREENSLEEVES
87876767

702   **I Am the Bread of Life**

me   un - less   the .. Fa - ther   beck - ons."
ev - er, ...   you   shall .. live   for - ev - er."
_blood,   you   shall   not have life   with - in   you."
die, ...   you   shall .. live   for - ev - er."
come   in - to ...... the .... world. ...

Refrain

"And I will raise you up, and I will raise you up,

and I will raise you up on the last day."

Text: John 6, adapt. S. Suzanne Toolan, SM, b. 1927
Music: S. Suzanne Toolan, SM, b. 1927
© 1966 GIA Publications, Inc.

I AM THE BREAD
irregular

703   Draw Us in the Spirit's Tether

1 Draw us in the Spir-it's teth-er, for when hum-bly
2 As dis-ci-ples used to gath-er in the name of
3 All our meals and all our liv-ing make as sac-ra-

in your name two or three are met to-geth-er,
Christ to sup, then with thanks to God the giv-er
ments of you, that by car-ing, help-ing, giv-ing,

you are in the midst of them. Al-le-lu-ia!
break the bread and bless the cup, Al-le-lu-ia!
we may be dis-ci-ples true. Al-le-lu-ia!

Al-le-lu-ia! Touch we now your gar-ment's hem.
Al-le-lu-ia! so now bind our friend-ship up.
Al-le-lu-ia! We will serve with faith a-new.

Text: Percy Dearmer, 1867-1936, alt.
Music: Harold Friedell, 1905-1958
Text © Oxford University Press, *Enlarged Songs of Praise*, 1931
Music © 1957, 1985 H. W. Gray, admin. CPP/Belwin

UNION SEMINARY
87878

alt. tune: PRAISE, MY SOU

Father, We Thank You

704

1 Fa - ther, we thank you that you plant - ed your ho - ly name with -
2 Watch o'er your Church, O Lord, in mer - cy, save it from e - vil,

in our hearts. Knowl - edge and faith and life im - mor - tal Je -
guard it still; per - fect it in your love, u - nite it, cleansed

sus your Son to us im - parts. Lord, you have made all for your
and con - formed un - to your will. As grain, once scat - tered on the

plea - sure, and giv'n us food for all our days, giv - ing in
hill - sides, was in this bro - ken bread made one, so from all

Christ the bread e - ter - nal; yours is the pow'r, yours be the praise.
lands your Church be gath - ered in - to your king - dom by your Son.

Text: *Didache*, 2nd cent., tr. F. Bland Tucker, 1895–1984, alt.
Music: attr. Louis Bourgeois, c. 1510–1561; arr. Claude Goudimel. 1505–1572, alt.
Tr. © 1940, 1943 The Church Pension Fund, ren. 1971, rev. 1985

RENDEZ À DIEU
9 8 9 8 D

705

As the Grains of Wheat

As the grains of wheat once scat-tered on the hill were gath-ered in-to
one to be-come our bread; so may all your peo-ple from
all the ends of earth be gath-ered in-to one in you.

1 As this cup of bless-ing is shared with-in our midst, ...
2 Let this be a fore-taste of all that is to come when

may we share the pres-ence of your love.
all cre-a-tion shares this feast with you.

Text: Marty Haugen, b. 1950
Music: Marty Haugen, b. 1950
© 1990 GIA Publications, Inc.

AS THE GRAINS
irregular

706 Eat This Bread, Drink This Cup

Refrain

Eat this bread, drink this cup. Taste and see the good-ness of God. Bread of life, cup of love, we re-joice in your pres-ence.

1 I will bless the Lord at all times,
2 Look up - on the Lord, be ra - diant,
3 An - gels fold their wings a - round us,
4 Saints of God, bow down and wor - ship,

praise with heart and voice; in my God I
nev - er turn a - way. God will save in
guard through good and ill. Those who seek the
bless the ho - ly name. Rise to tell God's

Refrain

glo - ry for - ev - er: lis - ten and re - joice!
ev - 'ry af - flic - tion, hear us when we pray.
Lord will lack noth - ing; taste, and have your fill.
great-ness for - ev - er, won - drous deeds pro - claim!

Text: Jeremy Young, b. 1948, refrain; *With One Voice*, 1995, stanzas (Ps. 34:1–10)
Music: Jeremy Young, b. 1948
© 1995 Augsburg Fortress

STONERIDGE
8 5 9 5 and refrain

707

This Is My Body

This is my bod - y giv - en up for you, this is my blood poured out for you. This is my bod - y giv - en up for you, this is my blood poured out for you.

Body of Christ. A - men. Blood of Christ. A - men. Body of Christ. A - men. Blood of Christ. A - men.

Text: Traditional
Music: Edward Bonnemère, b. 1921

CAUSE OF OUR JOY
irregular

Grains of Wheat
Una espiga

1 Grains of wheat, rich - ly gild - ed by the sun,
2 We en - joy true com - mun - ion in this meal,
3 As the grains join to form one loaf of bread,
4 We shall all sit to - geth - er at the feast

pur - ple clus - ters, col - lect - ed from the vine:
man - y grains God has plant - ed and made thrive;
as the notes come to - geth - er in one song,
shar - ing bread as God's chil - dren, joined in one:

these are al - tered, be - com - ing love's own bread and sweet wine,
like the grain we are ground be-neath life's sor - row - ful wheel,
as the rain - drops u - nite in - to the sin - gle vast sea,
in this hope we re - joice as we go for - ward in peace,

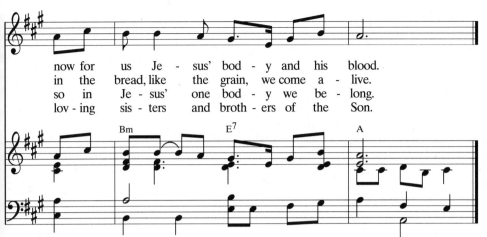

now for us Je - sus' bod - y and his blood.
in the bread, like the grain, we come a - live.
so in Je - sus' one bod - y we be - long.
lov - ing sis - ters and broth - ers of the Son.

1 Una espiga dorada por el sol,
  el racimo que corta el viñador,
  se convierten ahora en pan y vino de amor
  en el cuerpo y la sangre del Señor.

2 Comulgamos la misma comunión.
  Somos trigo del mismo sembrador.
  Un molino, la vida, nos tritura con dolor.
  Dios nos hace eucaristía en el amor.

3 Como granos que han hecho el mismo pan,
  como notas que tejen un cantar,
  como gotas de agua que se funden en el mar,
  los cristianos un cuerpo formarán.

4 En la mesa de Dios se sentarán,
  como hijos su pan compartirán,
  una misma esperanza caminando cantarán,
  en la vida como hermanos se amarán.

Text: Cesáreo Gabaraín, 1936–1991; tr. Madeleine Forell Marshall, b. 1946
Music: Cesáreo Gabaraín, 1936–1991; arr. Skinner Chávez-Melo, 1944–1992
Spanish text and music © 1973 Cesáreo Gabaraín, admin. OCP Publications
Tr. © 1995 Madeleine Forell Marshall, admin. Augsburg Fortress

UNA ESPIGA
10 10 13 10

Eat This Bread

709

Eat this bread, drink this cup, come to me and nev-er be hun - gry.

Eat this bread, drink this cup, trust in me and you will not thirst.

Text: John 6; adapt. Robert Batastini, b. 1942, and the Taizé Community
Music: Jacques Berthier, 1923–1994
© 1984 Les Presses de Taizé, admin. GIA Publications, Inc.

BERTHIER
irregular

710

One Bread, One Body

One bread, one bod-y, one Lord of all;

one cup of bless - ing which we bless,

and we, though man-y through-out the earth,

we are one bod - y in this one Lord.

1 Gen - tile or Jew, ser - vant or free,
2 Man - y the gifts, man - y the works,
3 Grain for the fields, scat-tered and grown,

wom - an or man, no more.
one in the Lord of all.
gath-ered to one for all.

Text: John Foley, SJ, b. 1939
Music: John Foley, SJ, b. 1939
© 1978, 1989 John B. Foley and New Dawn Music

ONE BREAD, ONE BODY
4 4 6 and refrain

You Satisfy the Hungry Heart

Gift of Finest Wheat

711

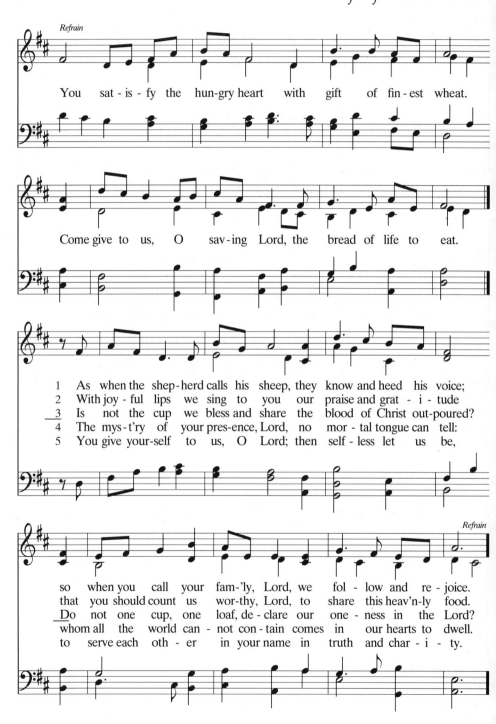

Refrain

You sat-is-fy the hun-gry heart with gift of fin-est wheat.

Come give to us, O sav-ing Lord, the bread of life to eat.

1 As when the shep-herd calls his sheep, they know and heed his voice;
2 With joy-ful lips we sing to you our praise and grat-i-tude
3 Is not the cup we bless and share the blood of Christ out-poured?
4 The mys-t'ry of your pres-ence, Lord, no mor-tal tongue can tell;
5 You give your-self to us, O Lord; then self-less let us be,

Refrain

so when you call your fam-'ly, Lord, we fol-low and re-joice.
that you should count us wor-thy, Lord, to share this heav'n-ly food.
Do not one cup, one loaf, de-clare our one-ness in the Lord?
whom all the world can-not con-tain comes in our hearts to dwell.
to serve each oth-er in your name in truth and char-i-ty.

Text: Omer Westendorf, b. 1916
Tune: Robert E. Kreutz, b. 1922
© 1977 Archdiocese of Philadelphia

BICENTENNIAL
C M and refrain

Listen, God Is Calling

Refrain
Leader / All

Lis - ten, lis - ten, God is call - ing through the Word in - vit - ing,

of - fer - ing for - give-ness, com - fort and joy. joy.

Leader / All

1 Je - sus gave his man - date: share the good news
2 Let none be for - got - ten through - out the world.
3 Help us to be faith - ful, stand - ing stead - fast,

Leader / All / *Refrain*

that he came to save us and set us free.
In the tri - une name of God go and bap - tize.
walk-ing in your pre - cepts, led by your Word.

Text: Tanzanian traditional, tr. Howard S. Olson, b. 1922
Music: Tanzanian tune, arr. Austin C. Lovelace, b. 1919
Tr. © Lutheran Theological College, Makumira, Tanzania
Arr. © Austin C. Lovelace

NENO LAKE MUNGU
6 4 6 4 and refrain

713 Lord, Let My Heart Be Good Soil

Lord, let my heart be good soil, o-pen to the seed of your Word. Lord, let my heart be good soil, where love can grow and peace is un-der-stood. When my heart is hard, break the stone a-way. When my heart is cold, warm it with the day. When my heart is lost, lead me on your way. Lord, let my heart,

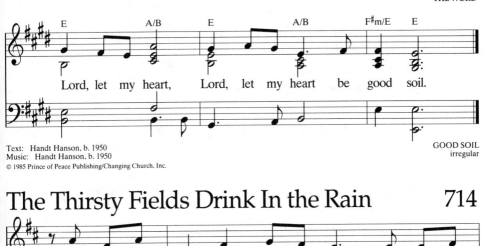

Lord, let my heart, Lord, let my heart be good soil.

Text: Handt Hanson, b. 1950
Music: Handt Hanson, b. 1950
© 1985 Prince of Peace Publishing/Changing Church, Inc.

GOOD SOIL
irregular

The Thirsty Fields Drink In the Rain   714

1 The thirst-y fields drink in the rain, the earth re-
2 The nurs-ing babe cries out for milk, the lit-tle
3 The dark-ness yearns for dawn to break, the flow-er
4 The pris-'ner longs to be set free, the fa-ther
5 We wait for you, O God, our Rock, we seek your

ceives the sow-er's seed and cov-ers it. So,
bird takes up a seed so she might live. So,
o-pens up its bud to face the sun. So,
runs to greet his son with o-pen arms. So,
light, your word, the truth we need to live. So,

Lord, we re-ceive your ho-ly Word.
Lord, we re-ceive your ho-ly Word.
Lord, we re-ceive your ho-ly Word.
Lord, we re-ceive your ho-ly Word.
Lord, send us now your ho-ly Word.

Text: Britt Hallqvist, b. 1914; tr. Gracia Grindal, b. 1943
Music: Mark Sedio, b. 1954
Tr. © 1994 Selah Publishing Co.
Music © 1995 Augsburg Fortress

CONVIVIO
8 8 4 9

715 Open Your Ears, O Faithful People

1 O - pen your ears, O faith-ful peo - ple, o - pen your ears and hear God's Word.
2 They who have ears to hear the mes-sage, they who have ears, now let them hear;
3 Is - ra - el comes to greet the Sav - ior, Ju - dah is glad to see his day,

O - pen your hearts, O roy - al priest-hood, God has come to you.
they who would learn the way of wis - dom, let them hear God's Word.
from east and west the peo-ples trav - el, God will show the way.

Refrain

God has spo - ken to the peo - ple,
To - rah o - ra, *To - rah o - ra,* hal - le - lu - jah!

Torah ora: The Law is light.

God has spo-ken words of wis-dom, hal-le-lu - jah!
To - rah o - ra, To - rah o - ra, hal - le - lu - jah!

God has spo-ken to the peo - ple, hal - le - lu - jah!
To - rah o - ra, To - rah o - ra, hal - le - lu - jah!

God has spo-ken words of wis-dom, hal - le - lu - jah!
To - rah o - ra, To - rah o - ra, hal - le - lu - jah!

Text: Hasidic traditional; English text, Willard F. Jabusch, b. 1930
Music: Hasidic tune; arr. *With One Voice,* 1995
Text © 1966, 1984 Willard F. Jabusch
Arr. © 1995 Augsburg Fortress

YISRAEL V'ORAITA
9 8 9 5 and refrain

716 Word of God, Come Down on Earth

1 Word of God, come down on earth, liv - ing rain from heav'n de-scend - ing; touch our hearts and bring to birth faith and hope and love un - end - ing. Word al-might - y, we re-vere you; Word made flesh, we long to hear you.

2 Word e - ter - nal, throned on high, Word that brought to life cre - a - tion, Word that came from heav'n to die, cru - ci - fied for our sal - va - tion, sav - ing Word, the world re-stor - ing, speak to us, your love out - pour - ing.

3 Word that caused blind eyes to see, speak and heal our mor - tal blind - ness; deaf we are: our heal - er be; loose our tongues to tell your kind - ness. Be our Word in pit - y spo - ken, heal the world, by our sin bro - ken.

4 Word that speaks God's ten - der love, one with God be - yond all tell - ing, Word that sends us from a - bove, God the Spir - it, with us dwell - ing, Word of truth, to all truth lead us; Word of life, with one bread feed us.

Text: James Quinn, SJ, b. 1919
Music: Johann R. Ahle, 1625–1673
Text © 1969 James Quinn, SJ, admin. Selah Publishing Co.

LIEBSTER JESU, WIR SIND HIER
787888

Come, All You People

Uyai mose

1 Come, all you peo - ple, come and praise the Most High;
1 U - ya - i mo - se, ti - na - ma - te Mwa - ri;
2 Come, all you peo - ple, come and praise the Sav - ior,
3 Come, all you peo - ple, come and praise the Spir - it,

come, all you peo - ple, come and praise the Most High;
u - ya - i mo - se, ti - na - ma - te Mwa - ri;
come, all you peo - ple, come and praise the Sav - ior,
come, all you peo - ple, come and praise the Spir - it,

come, all you peo - ple, come and praise the Most High;
u - ya - i mo - se, ti - na - ma - te Mwa - ri;
come, all you peo - ple, come and praise the Sav - ior,
come, all you peo - ple, come and praise the Spir - it,

come now and wor - ship the Lord.
u - ya - i mo - se Zvi - no.
come now and wor - ship the Lord.
come now and wor - ship the Lord.

Text: Alexander Gondo, Zimbabwe, 20th cent.; tr. I-to Loh, b. 1936; *With One Voice*, 1995, st. 2–3
Music: Alexander Gondo
© 1986 World Council of Churches

UYAI MOSE
5 6 5 6 5 6 7

Here in This Place
Gather Us In

718

1 Here in this place . . . new light is stream-ing, now is the dark-ness
2 We are the young, our lives are a mys-t'ry, we are the old who
3 Here we will take the wine and the wa-ter, here we will take the
4 Not in the dark of build-ings con-fin - ing, not in some heav - en,

van - ished a - way; see in this space our fears and our dream-ings
yearn for your face; we have been sung through-out all of his - t'ry,
bread of new birth, here you shall call your sons and your daugh-ters,
light years a - way— here in this place the new light is shin - ing,

brought here to you in the light of this day.
called to be light to the whole hu-man race.
call us a - new to be salt for the earth.
now is the king-dom, and now is the day.

Text: Marty Haugen, b. 1950
Music: Marty Haugen, b. 1950
© 1982 GIA Publications, Inc.

GATHER US IN
10 9 10 10 D

719

God Is Here!

1 God is here! As we your peo-ple meet to of-fer
2 Here are sym-bols to re-mind us of our life - long
3 Here our chil-dren find a wel-come in the Shep-herd's
4 Lord of all, of Church and king-dom, in an age of

praise and prayer, may we find in full - er mea-sure
need of grace; here are ta - ble, font, and pul-pit;
flock and fold; here as bread and wine are tak-en,
change and doubt keep us faith - ful to the Gos-pel;

what it is in Christ we share. Here, as in the
here the cross has cen - tral place. Here in hon - es -
Christ sus - tains us, as of old. Here the ser - vants
help us work your pur - pose out. Here, in this day's

world a - round us, all our var - ied skills and arts
ty of preach-ing, here in si - lence, as in speech,
of the Ser - vant seek in wor - ship to ex - plore
ded - i - ca - tion, all we have to give, re - ceive;

wait the com-ing of the Spir-it in-to o-pen minds and hearts.
here, in new-ness and re-new-al, God the Spir-it comes to each.
what it means in dai-ly liv-ing to be-lieve and to a-dore.
we, who can-not live with-out you, we a-dore you! We be-lieve!

Text: Fred Pratt Green, b. 1903
Music: Cyril V. Taylor, 1907–1991
Text © 1979 Hope Publishing Co.; music © 1942, ren. 1970 Hope Publishing Co.

ABBOT'S LEIGH
8 7 8 7 D

In the Presence of Your People 720

In the pres-ence of your peo-ple I will praise your name,

for a-lone you are ho-ly, en-throned on the prais-es of Is-ra-el.

Let us cel-e-brate your good-ness and your stead-fast love;

may your name be ex-alt-ed here on earth and in heav'n a-bove.

Text: Brent Chambers, b. 1948
Music: Brent Chambers, b. 1948
© 1977 Scripture in Song, admin. Maranatha Music c/o The Copyright Co.

THE CELEBRATION SONG
irregular

721 Go, My Children, with My Blessing

1 "Go, my chil - dren, with my bless - ing, nev - er a - lone.
2 "Go, my chil - dren, sins for - giv - en, at peace and pure.
3 "Go, my chil - dren, fed and nour - ished, clos - er to me.
4 "I the Lord will bless and keep you, and give you peace.

Wak - ing, sleep - ing, I am with you, you are my own.
Here you learned how much I love you, what I can cure.
Grow in love and love by serv - ing, joy - ful and free.
I the Lord will smile up - on you, and give you peace.

In my love's bap - tis - mal riv - er I have made you mine for - ev - er.
Here you heard my dear Son's sto - ry, here you touched him, saw his glo - ry.
Here my Spir - it's pow - er filled you, here my ten - der com-fort stilled you.
I the Lord will be your Fa - ther, Sav - ior, Com - fort - er and Broth - er.

Go, my chil - dren, with my bless - ing, you are my own."
Go, my chil - dren, sins for - giv - en, at peace and pure."
Go, my chil - dren, fed and nour - ished, joy - ful and free."
Go, my chil - dren, I will keep you, and give you peace."

Text: Jaroslav Vajda, b. 1919
Music: Welsh
Text © 1983 Jaroslav J. Vajda

AR HYD Y NOS
84848884

Hallelujah! We Sing Your Praises

Each refrain and stanza is sung twice in succession.

Text: South African
Music: South African
© 1984 Utryck. admin. Walton Music Corp.

HALELUYA! PELO TSO RONA
irregular

723 The Spirit Sends Us Forth to Serve

1 The Spir - it sends us forth to serve; we go in
2 We go to com - fort those who mourn and set the
3 We go to be the hands of Christ, to scat - ter
4 Then let us go to serve in peace, the Gos - pel

Je - sus' name to bring glad tid - ings
bur - dened free; where hope is dim, to
joy like seed and, all our days, to
to pro - claim. God's Spir - it has em -

to the poor, God's fa - vor to pro - claim.
share a dream and help the blind to see.
cher - ish life, to do the lov - ing deed.
pow - er'd us; we go in Je - sus' name.

Text: Delores Dufner, OSB, b. 1939
Music: Thomas Haweis, 1734-1820
Text © 1993 Delores Dufner, OSB, admin. OCP Publications

CHESTERFIELD
C M

724 Shalom

Canon: 1   Dm   2   3   Am   Dm

Sha-lom, my friends, sha - lom, my friends, sha - lom, sha - lom.
Sha-lom cha - ve - rim, sha - lom cha - ve - rim, sha - lom, sha - lom.

Dm   Am   Dm   Am   Dm

Sha-lom, my friends, sha - lom, my friends, sha - lom, sha - lom.
Sha-lom cha - ve - rim, sha - lom cha - ve - rim, sha - lom, sha - lom.

Text: Israeli traditional
Music: Israeli traditional

SHALOM
irregular

Blessed Be the God of Israel 725

1 Bless'd be the God of Is - ra - el who comes to set us free
2 With prom-ised mer - cy will God still the cov - e - nant re - call,
3 My child, as proph-et of the Lord you will pre-pare the way,

and rais - es up new hope for us: a Branch from Da - vid's tree.
the oath once sworn to A - bra-ham, from foes to save us all;
to tell God's peo - ple they are saved from sin's e - ter - nal sway.

So have the proph-ets long de-clared that with a might-y arm
that we might wor - ship with-out fear and of - fer lives of praise,
Then shall God's mer - cy from on high shine forth and nev - er cease

God would turn back our en - e - mies and all who wish us harm.
in ho - li - ness and righ - teous-ness to serve God all our days.
to drive a - way the gloom of death and lead us in - to peace.

Text: Carl P. Daw, Jr., b. 1944
Music: English folk tune, arr. Ralph Vaughan Williams, 1872–1958
Text © 1989 Hope Publishing Co.
Music from *The English Hymnal*, © 1906 Oxford University Press

FOREST GREEN
CMD

Oh, Sing to God Above
Cantemos al Señor

1 Oh, sing to God a - bove a hymn of joy - ful greet-ing,
2 Oh, sing to God a - bove a hymn of praise and bless-ing,
1 Can-te - mos al Se - ñor un him - no de_a - le - grí - a,
2 Can-te - mos al Se - ñor un him - no de_a - la - ban - za

a song of grate-ful love in the new day's light re - peat-ing:
a song of grate-ful love, hope and faith our hearts ex - press-ing:
un cán - ti - co de_a-mor al na - cer el nue - vo dí - a.
que_ex-pre - se nues-tro_a-mor, nues-tra fe y nues-tra_es-pe - ran - za.

you made the sea and sky, the sun and stars in splen-dor;
cre - a - tion lifts its voice to tell your might and glo - ry,
El hi - zo_el cie - lo, el mar, el sol y las es - tre - llas
En to - da la crea - ción pre - go - na su gran-de - za,

de- light shone in your eye— all your works were filled with won-der.
and we, too, will re - joice to pro-claim the sav - ing sto - ry,
y vio_en e - llos bon - dad, pues sus o - bras e - ran be - llas.
a - sí nues-tro can - tar va_a-nun - cian - do su be - lle - za.

Text: Carlos Rosas, b. 1939; tr. *With One Voice*, 1995
Music: Carlos Rosas, b. 1939; arr. Raquel Mora Martinez
Spanish text and tune © 1976 Resource Publications, Inc.; tr. © 1995 Augsburg Fortress
Arr. © 1983 The United Methodist Publishing House

ROSAS
6 7 6 8 D and refrain

Lord, Your Hands Have Formed 727

1 Lord, your hands have formed this world, ev - 'ry part is
2 Yours the soil that holds the seed, you give warmth and
3 Like a mat you roll out land, space to build for

shaped by you — wa - ter tum - bling o - ver rocks, air and
mois - ture, too. Sprout - ing blos - soms, crops and buds, trees and
us and you earth - ly homes and, bet - ter still, homes for

sun - light: each day's signs that you make all things new.
plants: the sea - son's signs that you make all things new.
Christ: the tru - est sign that you make all things new.

Text: Ramon and Sario Aliano, tr. Delbert Rice, para. James Minchin
Music: Ikalahan (Philippines) traditional
Text © James Minchin, admin. Asian Institute for Liturgy & Music

GAYOM NI HIGAMI
7 7 7 7 6

728   O Light Whose Splendor Thrills

1 O Light whose splen - dor thrills and glad - dens
2 As twi - light hov - ers near at sun - set,
3 In all life's bril - liant, time - less mo - ments,

with ra - diance bright - er than the sun,
and lamps are lit, and chil - dren nod,
let faith - ful voic - es sing your praise,

pure gleam of God's un - end - ing glo - ry,
in eve - ning hymns we lift our voic - es
O Son of God, our life - be - stow - er,

O Je - sus, blest A - noint - ed One:
to Fa - ther, Spir - it, Son, one God.
whose glo - ry light - ens end - less days.

Text: Greek hymn, 3rd cent.; para. Carl P. Daw, Jr., b. 1944
Music: Clement Scholefield, 1839–1904
Text © 1989 Hope Publishing Co.

ST. CLEMENT
9 8 9 8

Christ, Mighty Savior

729

1 Christ, might-y Sav - ior, Light of all cre - a - tion, you make the
2 Now comes the day's end as the sun is set - ting: mir - ror of
3 There - fore we come now eve - ning rites to of - fer, joy - ful - ly
4 Give heed, we pray you, to our sup - pli - ca - tion: that you may
5 Though bod - ies slum - ber, hearts shall keep their vig - il, for - ev - er

day - time ra - diant with the sun - light and to the night give
day - break, pledge of res - ur - rec - tion; while in the heav - ens
chant - ing ho - ly hymns to praise you, with all cre - a - tion
grant us par - don for of - fens - es, strength for our weak hearts,
rest - ing in the peace of Je - sus, in light or dark - ness

glit - ter - ing a - dorn - ment, stars in the heav - ens.
choirs of stars ap - pear - ing hal - low the night - fall.
join - ing hearts and voic - es, sing - ing your glo - ry.
rest for ach - ing bod - ies, sooth - ing the wea - ry.
wor - ship - ing our Sav - ior now and for - ev - er.

Text: Mozarabic, 10th cent.; tr. Alan McDougall, 1895–1964 and Anne LeCroy, b. 1930
Music: Richard W. Dirksen, b. 1921
Tr. © 1982 The United Methodist Publishing House
Music © 1984 Richard W. Dirksen

INNISFREE FARM
11 11 11 5

alt. tune: CHRISTE SANCTORUM

730 My Soul Proclaims Your Greatness

1 My soul pro-claims your great-ness, Lord; I sing my Sav-ior's praise!
2 To all who live in ho-ly fear your mer-cy ev-er flows.
3 To Is-ra-el, your ser-vant blest, your help is ev-er sure;

You looked up-on my low-li-ness, and I am full of grace.
With might-y arm you dash the proud, their schem-ing hearts ex-pose.
the prom-ise to our par-ents made their chil-dren will se-cure.

Now ev-'ry land and ev-'ry age this bless-ing shall pro-claim—
The ruth-less you have cast a-side, the low-ly throned in-stead;
Sing glo-ry to the Ho-ly One, give hon-or to the Word,

great won-ders you have done for me, and ho-ly is your name.
the hun-gry filled with all good things, the rich sent off un-fed.
and praise the Pow'r of the Most High, one God, by all a-dored.

Text: Luke 1:46–55; tr. *With One Voice*, 1995
Music: English melody, arr. Ralph Vaughan Williams, 1872–1958
Text © 1995 Augsburg Fortress

KINGSFOLD
C M D

Precious Lord, Take My Hand

731

Text: George N. Allen, *The Oberlin Social and Sabbath School Hymn Book*, 1844; adapt. Thomas A. Dorsey, 1899–1993
Music: Thomas A. Dorsey, 1899–1993

PRECIOUS LORD
irregular

732

Create in Me a Clean Heart

Cre - ate in me a clean heart, O God, and re - new a right spir-it with - in me. Cast me not a - way from your pres-ence, and take not your Ho - ly Spir - it from me. Re - store to me the joy of your sal - va -tion, and up - hold me with your free Spir - it.

Text: Psalm 51:10–12
Music: J.A. Freylinghausen, 1670–1739, arr. Harold W. Gilbert
Arr. © 1958 *Service Book and Hymnal*

FRANCKE
irregular

Our Father, We Have Wandered

733

1 Our Fa - ther, we have wan - dered and hid - den from your face;
2 And now at length dis - cern - ing the e - vil that we do,
3 O Lord of all the liv - ing, both ban - ished and re - stored,

in fool - ish - ness have squan - dered your leg - a - cy of grace.
be - hold us, Lord, re - turn - ing with hope and trust to you.
com - pas - sion - ate, for - giv - ing and ev - er - car - ing Lord,

But now, in ex - ile dwell - ing, we rise with fear and shame,
In haste you come to meet us and home re - joic - ing bring,
grant now that our trans - gress - ing, our faith - less - ness may cease.

as, dis - tant but com - pel - ling, we hear you call our name.
in glad - ness there to greet us with calf and robe and ring.
Stretch out your hand in bless - ing, in par - don, and in peace.

Text: Kevin Nichols, b. 1929
Music: Hans Leo Hassler, 1564–1612; arr. J.S. Bach, 1685–1750
Text © 1981, International Committee on English in the Liturgy, Inc.

HERZLICH TUT MICH VERLANGEN
7 6 7 6 D

734 Softly and Tenderly Jesus Is Calling

1 Soft - ly and ten - der - ly Je - sus is call - ing,
2 Why should we tar - ry when Je - sus is plead - ing,
3 Oh, for the won - der - ful love he has prom - ised,

call - ing for you and for me. See, on the por - tals he's
plead-ing for you and for me? Why should we lin - ger and
prom-ised for you and for me! Though we have sinned, he has

wait-ing and watch-ing, watch-ing for you and for me.
heed not his mer - cies, mer - cies for you and for me?
mer - cy and par - don, par - don for you and for me.

Refrain

"Come home, come home! You who are
Come home, come home!

wea-ry, come home." Ear-nest-ly, ten-der-ly,

Je - sus is call - ing, call-ing, "O sin-ner, come home!"

Text: Will Thompson, 1847–1909
Music: Will Thompson, 1847–1909

THOMPSON
11 7 11 7 and refrain

God! When Human Bonds Are Broken 735

1 God!   When hu-man bonds are bro-ken and we lack the love or skill
2 Through that still-ness, with your Spir-it come in-to our world of stress,
3 You   in   us are bruised and bro-ken: hear us as we seek re-lease
4 Send   us, God of new   be-gin-nings, hum-bly hope-ful in-to life.
5 Give   us faith to be   more faith-ful, give us hope to be more true,

to   re-store the   hope of heal-ing, give us grace and make us still.
for the sake of   Christ for-giv-ing   all the fail-ures we con-fess.
from the pain of   ear-lier liv-ing;   set us free and grant us peace.
Use us as a   means of bless-ing: make us stron-ger, give us faith.
give us love to   go on learn-ing: God! En-cour-age and re-new!

Text: Fred Kaan, b. 1929
Music: William H. Monk, 1823–1889
Text © 1989 Hope Publishing Co.

MERTON
8 7 8 7

alt. tune: OMNI DIE

736

By Gracious Powers

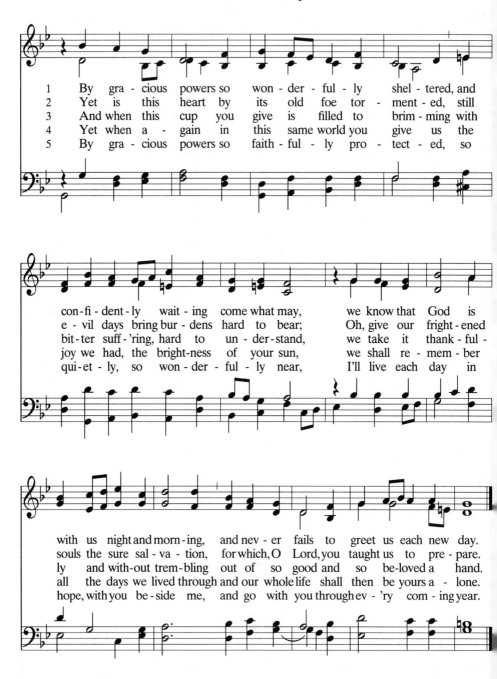

1 By gra - cious powers so won - der - ful - ly shel - tered, and
2 Yet is this heart by its old foe tor - ment - ed, still
3 And when this cup you give is filled to brim - ming with
4 Yet when a - gain in this same world you give us the
5 By gra - cious powers so faith - ful - ly pro - tect - ed, so

con - fi - dent - ly wait - ing come what may, we know that God is
e - vil days bring bur - dens hard to bear; Oh, give our fright - ened
bit - ter suff - 'ring, hard to un - der-stand, we take it thank - ful -
joy we had, the bright-ness of your sun, we shall re - mem - ber
qui - et - ly, so won - der - ful - ly near, I'll live each day in

with us night and morn - ing, and nev - er fails to greet us each new day.
souls the sure sal - va - tion, for which, O Lord, you taught us to pre - pare.
ly and with-out trem - bling out of so good and so be-loved a hand.
all the days we lived through and our whole life shall then be yours a - lone.
hope, with you be - side me, and go with you through ev - 'ry com - ing year.

Text: Dietrich Bonhöffer, 1906–1945; tr. Fred Pratt Green, b. 1903
Music: Janet Hill, b. 1944
Tr. © 1974 Hope Publishing Co.
Music © 1995 Augsburg Fortress

BERLIN
11 10 11 10

alt. tune: INTERCESSOR

There Is a Balm in Gilead

Refrain

There is a balm in Gil-e-ad to make the wound-ed whole;

there is a balm in Gil-e-ad to heal the sin-sick soul.

1 Some-times I feel dis - cour-aged and think my work's in vain,
2 If you can - not preach like Pe - ter, if you can - not pray like Paul,
3 Don't ev - er feel dis - cour-aged, for Je - sus is your friend;

but then the Ho - ly Spir - it re - vives my soul a - gain.
you can tell the love of Je - sus and say, "He died for all."
and if you lack for knowl-edge he'll ne'er re-fuse to lend.

Text: African American spiritual
Music: African American spiritual

BALM IN GILEAD
irregular

738

Healer of Our Every Ill

1 You who know our fears and sad - ness,
2 In the pain and joy be - hold - ing
3 Give us strength to love each oth - er,
4 You who know each thought and feel - ing,

grace us with your peace and glad - ness; Spir - it of all
how your grace is still un - fold - ing, give us all your
ev - 'ry sis - ter, ev - 'ry broth - er; Spir - it of all
teach us all your way of heal - ing; Spir - it of com -

Refrain

com - fort, fill our hearts.
vi - sion, God of love.
kind - ness, be our guide.
pas - sion, fill each heart.

Text: Marty Haugen, b. 1950
Music: Marty Haugen, b. 1950
© 1987 GIA Publications, Inc.

HEALER OF OUR EVERY ILL
8 8 9 and refrain

739   In All Our Grief

1 In all our grief and fear we turn to you. O God, you know all
2 Help us to put a - side the an - gry word, the clench-ing fist, the
3 You did not e - ven spare your on - ly Son. He lived our griefs and
4 God, when we suf - fer all that we can bear, then let us know that

that we think or do, you know the pain we put each oth - er through.
wish and will to hurt. Teach us the way in which love best is served.
bore all e - vil done, but through his cross, re - demp-tion has been won.
you in truth are near and will not leave us lost in all our fear.

Refrain

Lord, have mer - cy, Christ have mer - cy, Lord, grant us peace.

Text: Sylvia Dunstan, 1955–1993
Music: Charles R. Anders, b. 1929
Text © 1991 GIA Publications, Inc.; music © 1978 *Lutheran Book of Worship*

FREDERICKTOWN
10 10 10 and refrain

740   Jesus, Remember Me

Je - sus, re - mem-ber me when you come in - to your king-dom.

Je - sus, re - mem-ber me when you come in - to your king - dom.

Text: Luke 23:42
Music: Jacques Berthier, 1923–1994
© 1981 Les Presses de Taizé, admin. GIA Publications, Inc.

REMEMBER ME
irregular

Thy Holy Wings

741

1 Thy ho-ly wings O Sav-ior, spread gent-ly o-ver me
2 Oh, let me nes-tle near thee, with-in thy down-y breast
3 Oh, wash me in the wa-ters of No-ah's cleans-ing flood.

and let me rest se-cure-ly through good and ill in thee.
where I will find sweet com-fort and peace with-in thy nest.
Give me a will-ing spir-it, a heart both clean and good.

Oh, be my strength and por-tion, my rock and hid-ing place,
Oh, close thy wings a-round me and keep me safe-ly there,
Oh, take in-to thy keep-ing thy child-ren great and small,

and let my ev-'ry mo-ment be lived with-in thy grace.
for I am but a new-born and need thy ten-der care.
and while we sweet-ly slum-ber, en-fold us one and all.

Text: Carolina Sandell-Berg, 1832–1903, st. 1,3; Gracia Grindal, b. 1943, st. 2 and tr., st. 1, 3
Music: Swedish folk tune, arr. *With One Voice*, 1995
English text © 1983 Gracia Grindal
Arr. © 1995 Augsburg Fortress

BRED DINA VIDA VINGAR
7 6 7 6 D

742

Come, We That Love the Lord

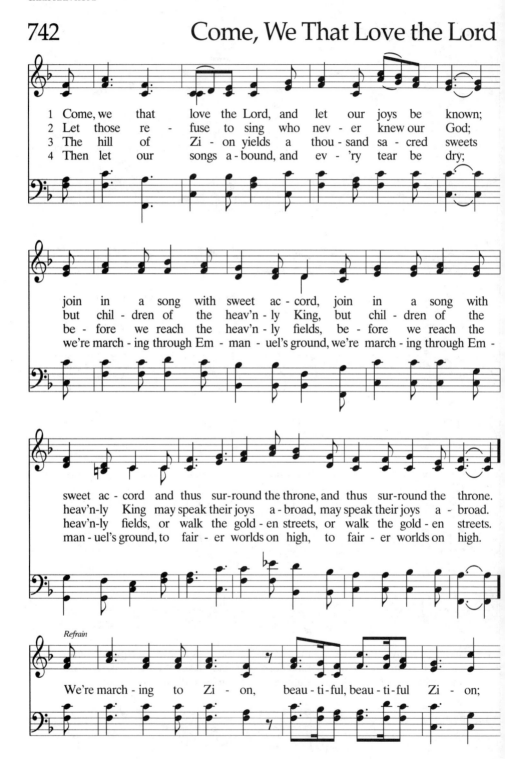

1 Come, we that love the Lord, and let our joys be known;
2 Let those re - fuse to sing who nev - er knew our God;
3 The hill of Zi - on yields a thou - sand sa - cred sweets
4 Then let our songs a - bound, and ev - 'ry tear be dry;

join in a song with sweet ac - cord, join in a song with
but chil - dren of the heav'n - ly King, but chil - dren of the
be - fore we reach the heav'n - ly fields, be - fore we reach the
we're march - ing through Em - man - uel's ground, we're march - ing through Em -

sweet ac - cord and thus sur-round the throne, and thus sur-round the throne.
heav'n-ly King may speak their joys a - broad, may speak their joys a - broad.
heav'n-ly fields, or walk the gold - en streets, or walk the gold - en streets.
man - uel's ground, to fair - er worlds on high, to fair - er worlds on high.

Refrain

We're march - ing to Zi - on, beau - ti - ful, beau - ti - ful Zi - on;

we're march-ing up-ward to Zi - on, the beau-ti-ful cit-y of God.

Text: Isaac Watts, 1674–1748, stanzas; Robert Lowry, 1826–1899, refrain
Music: Robert Lowry, 1826–1899

MARCHING TO ZION
6 6 8 8 6 6 and refrain

Stay with Us   743

1 Stay with us, till night has come: our praise to
2 Walk with us, our spir-its sigh: hear when our
3 Walk with us, the road will bend: make all our
4 Talk with us, till we be - hold a joy - ful
5 Stay with us, till day is done: no tears nor

you this day be sung. Bless our bread, o - pen our
wear - y spir - its cry, feel a - gain our loss, our
weep-ing, wail - ing end. Wipe our tears, for - give our
life you will un - fold: heal our eyes to see the
dark shall dim the sun. Cheer the heart, your grace im -

eyes: Je - sus, be our great sur - prise.
pain: Je - sus, take us to your side.
fears: Je - sus, lift the heav - y cross.
prize: Je - sus, take us to the light.
part: Je - sus, bring e - ter - nal life.

Text: Herbert F. Brokering, b. 1926
Music: Walter L. Pelz, b. 1926
© 1990 Concordia Publishing House

STAY WITH US
7 8 7 7

744

Soon and Very Soon

1 Soon and ver - y soon
2 No more cry - in' there   we are goin' to see the King,
3 No more dy - in' there
4 Soon and ver - y soon

soon and ver - y soon
no more cry - in' there   we are goin' to see the King,
no more dy - in' there
soon and ver - y soon

soon and ver - y soon
no more cry - in' there   we are goin' to see the King.
no more dy - in' there
soon and ver - y soon

Refrain

Hal-le - lu - jah, hal-le - lu - jah, we're goin' to see the King!

Hal - le - lu - jah, hal - le - lu -
jah, hal - le - lu - jah, hal - le - lu - jah.

Text: Andraé Crouch, b. 1942
Music: Andraé Crouch, b. 1942
© 1976 Budjohn Songs/Crouch Music, admin. The Sparrow Corp.

VERY SOON
12 12 12 and refrain

Awake, O Sleeper 745

1 A - wake, O sleep - er, rise from death, and Christ shall give you light;
2 To us on earth he came to bring from sin and fear re - lease,
3 Then walk in love as Christ has loved, who died that he might save;
4 For us Christ lived, for us he died, and con - quered in the strife.

so learn his love, its length and breadth, its full - ness, depth, and height.
to give the Spir - it's u - ni - ty, the ver - y bond of peace.
with kind and gen - tle hearts for - give as God in Christ for - gave.
A - wake, a - rise, go forth in faith, and Christ shall give you life.

Text: F. Bland Tucker, 1895–1984
Music: Carl G. Gläser, 1784–1829
Text © 1980 Augsburg Publishing House

AZMON
C M

746

Day by Day

1 Day by day, your mer-cies, Lord, at-tend me, bring-ing com-fort
2 Day by day, I know you will pro-vide me strength to serve and
3 Oh, what joy to know that you are near me when my bur-dens

to my anx-ious soul. Day by day, the bless-ings, Lord, you send me
wis-dom to o-bey; I will seek your lov-ing will to guide me
grow too great to bear; oh, what joy to know that you will hear me

draw me near-er to my heav'n-ly goal. Love di-vine, be-yond all
o'er the paths I strug-gle day by day. I will fear no e-vil
when I come, O Lord, to you in prayer. Day by day, no mat-ter

mor-tal meas-ure, brings to naught the bur-dens of my quest; Sav-ior,
of the mor-row, I will trust in your en-dur-ing grace. Sav-ior,
what be-tide me, you will hold me ev-er in your hand. Sav-ior,

lead me to the home I trea-sure, where at last I'll find e-ter-nal rest.
help me bear life's pain and sor-row till in glo-ry I be-hold your face.
with your pres-ence here to guide me, I will reach at last the prom-ised land.

Text: Carolina Sandell Berg, 1832–1903; tr. Robert Leaf, b. 1936
Music: Oskar Ahnfelt, 1813–1882
Tr. © 1992 Augsburg Fortress

BLOTT EN DAG
10 9 10 9 D

Christ Is Made the Sure Foundation 747

1 Christ is made the sure foun-da - tion, Christ, our head and
2 To this tem - ple, where we call you, come, O Lord of
3 Grant, we pray, to all your faith - ful all the gifts they
4 Praise and hon - or to the Fa - ther, praise and hon - or

cor - ner - stone, cho - sen of the Lord and pre - cious,
hosts, and stay; come with all your lov - ing - kind - ness,
ask to gain; what they gain from you, for - ev - er
to the Son, praise and hon - or to the Spir - it,

bind - ing all the Church in one; ho - ly Zi - on's
hear your peo - ple as they pray; and your full - est
with the bless - ed to re - tain; and here - af - ter
ev - er three and ev - er one: one in might and

help for - ev - er and our con - fi - dence a - lone.
ben - e - dic - tion shed with - in these walls to - day.
in your glo - ry ev - er - more with you to reign.
one in glo - ry while un - end - ing a - ges run!

Text: Latin hymn, c. 7th cent.; tr. John M. Neale, 1818–1866, alt.
Music: Henry Purcell, 1659–1695; arr. Ernest Hawkins, 1802–1868

WESTMINSTER ABBEY
878787

748

Bind Us Together

Bind us to-geth-er, Lord, bind us to-geth-er with cords that can-not be bro-ken. Bind us to-geth-er, Lord, bind us to-geth-er, Lord; bind us to-geth-er in love.

1 There . . is on-ly one God. There . . is on-ly one King.
2 You are the fam-'ly of God. You are the prom-ise di - vine.

There . . is on-ly one Bod-y; that . . is why we can sing:
You are God's cho-sen de - sire, you are the glo-rious new wine.

Text: Bob Gillman, b. 1946
Music: Bob Gillman, b. 1946
© 1977 Thankyou Music, admin. (in Western Hemisphere) Integrity's Hosanna! Music

BIND US TOGETHER
6 7 7 6 and refrain

When Love Is Found

749

1 When love is found and hope comes home, sing and be glad that two are one. When love ex - plodes and fills the sky, praise God and share our mak - er's joy.

2 When love has flow'red in trust and care, build both each day that love may dare to reach be - yond home's warmth and light, to serve and strive for truth and right.

3 When love is tried as loved-ones change, hold still to hope though all seems strange, till ease re - turns and love grows wise through list - 'ning ears and o - pened eyes.

4 When love is torn and trust be - trayed, pray strength to love till tor - ments fade, till lov - ers keep no score of wrong but hear through pain love's Eas - ter song.

5 Praise God for love, praise God for life, in age or youth, in hus - band, wife. Lift up your hearts. Let love be fed through death and life in bro - ken bread.

Text: Brian Wren, b. 1936
Music: English tune; arr. Carolyn Jennings, b. 1936
Text © 1983 by Hope Publishing Co.
Arr. © 1995 Augsburg Fortress

O WALY WALY
L M

750   Oh, Praise the Gracious Power

1 Oh, praise the gra-cious power that tum-bles walls of fear
2 Oh, praise per-sis-tent truth that o-pens fist-ed minds
3 Oh, praise in-clu-sive love, en-cir-cling ev-'ry race,
4 Oh, praise the word of faith that claims us as God's own,
5 Oh, praise the tide of grace that laps at ev-'ry shore

and gath-ers in one house of faith all stran-gers far and near:
and eas-es from their anx-ious clutch the prej-u-dice that blinds:
ob-liv-i-ous to gen-der, wealth, to so-cial rank or place:
a liv-ing tem-ple built on Christ, our rock and cor-ner-stone:
with vi-sions of a world at peace, no long-er bled by war:

Refrain

We praise you, Christ! Your cross has made us one!

6 Oh, praise the power, the truth,
   the love, the word, the tide.
   Yet more than these, oh, praise their source,
   praise Christ the crucified. *Refrain*

7 Oh, praise the living Christ
   with faith's bright songful voice!
   Announce the Gospel to the world
   and with these words rejoice: *Refrain*

Text: Thomas H. Troeger, b. 1945
Music: Carol Doran, b. 1936
© 1986 Oxford University Press, Inc.

CHRISTPRAISE RAY
S M and refrain

As Man and Woman We Were Made 751

1 As man and wom - an we were made that love be found and
2 Now Je - sus lived and gave his love to make our life and
3 And Je - sus died to live a - gain, so praise the love that,
4 Then spread the ta - ble, clear the hall, and cel - e - brate till

life be - gun, so praise the Lord who made us two, and
lov - ing new; so cel - e - brate with him to - day and
come what may, can bring the dawn and clear the skies, and
day is done; let peace go deep be - tween us all and

praise the Lord when two are one: praise for the love that
drink the joy he of - fers you, that makes the sim - ple
waits to wipe all tears a - way; and let us hope for
joy be shared by ev - 'ry - one; laugh and make mer - ry

comes to life through child or par - ent, hus - band, wife.
mo - ment shine and chang - es wa - ter in - to wine.
what shall be, be - liev - ing where we can - not see.
with your friends, and praise the love that nev - er ends.

Text: Brian Wren, b. 1936
Music: English tune, arr. Ralph Vaughan Williams, 1872–1958
Text © 1983 Hope Publishing Co.

SUSSEX CAROL
888888

I, the Lord of Sea and Sky

Here I Am, Lord

1 "I, the Lord of sea and sky,
2 "I, the Lord of snow and rain,
3 "I, the Lord of wind and flame,

I have heard my peo-ple cry.
I have borne my peo-ple's pain.
I will tend the poor and lame.

All who dwell in deep-est sin
I have wept for love of them.
I will set a feast for them.

my hand will save.
They turn a - way.
My hand will save.

I, who made the stars of night,
I will break their hearts of stone,
Fin-est bread I will pro-vide

I will make their dark-ness bright.
give them hearts for love a - lone.
till their hearts be sat - is - fied.

Who will bear my light to them? Whom shall I send?"
I will speak my word to them. Whom shall I send?"
I will give my life to them. Whom shall I send?"

Refrain

Here I am, Lord. Is it I, Lord? I have heard you call-ing in the night. I will go, Lord, if you lead me. I will hold your peo-ple in my heart.

Text: Daniel Schutte
Music: Daniel Schutte; arr. Michael Pope, SJ, Daniel L. Schutte, and John Weissrock
© 1981 Daniel L. Schutte and New Dawn Music

HERE I AM, LORD
7 7 7 4 D and refrain

You Are the Seed
Sois la semilla

753

1 You are the seed that will grow a new sprout; you're a star that will
2 You are the flame that will light-en the dark, so re-splen-dent with
3 You are the life that will nur-ture the plant; you're the waves in a

shine in the night; you are the yeast and a small grain of salt, a
hope, faith and love; you are the shep-herds to lead the whole world to
tur-bu-lent sea; yes-ter-day's yeast is be-gin-ning to rise, a

bea-con to glow in the dark. You are the dawn that will
wa-ters and pas-tures of peace. "You are the friends that I
new loaf of bread it will yield. There is no place for a

bring a new day; you're the wheat that will bear gold-en grain;
chose for my-self, you're the word that I want to pro-claim.
cit-y to hide, there's no moun-tain can cov-er its might;

you are a sting and a soft, gen-tle touch, to wit-ness where-
You are the new reign of God built on rock, where jus-tice and
let your light shine so that your lov-ing works give hon-or and

ev - er you go.   Go, my friends, go to the world, pro -
truth are at home."   Be, my friends, a loy - al wit - ness,
glo - ry to God.   *Id, a - mi - gos, por el mun - do,*
              Sed, a - mi - gos, mis tes - ti - gos

claim the great love of God; mes - sen-gers to tell the way of life,
from the dead Christ a - rose; "Lo, I'll be with you for - ev - er-more,
a - nun-cian-do_el a - mor,   men - sa - je-ros de la vi - da,
de mi re - su - rrec - ción.   Id lle-van-do mi pre-sen - cia;

peace and par - don for all.   till the end of the world."
de la paz y el per - dón.   con vo - so - tros es - toy.

Text: Cesáreo Gabaraín, 1936–1991; tr. Raquel Gutiérrez-Achon, b. 1927 and Skinner Chávez-Melo, 1944–1992, alt.   ID Y ENSEÑAD
Music: Cesáreo Gabaraín, 1936–1991; arr. Skinner Chávez-Melo, 1944–1992   10 9 10 8 D and refrain
Text & tune © 1979 Ediciones Paulinas, admin. OCP Publications; tr. © The United Methodist Publishing House
Arr. © 1987 Estate of Skinner Chávez-Melo

754   Let Us Talents and Tongues Employ

1 Let us tal - ents and tongues em - ploy, reach-ing out with a shout of joy:
2 Christ is a - ble to make us one, at the ta - ble he sets the tone,
3 Je - sus calls us in, sends us out bear-ing fruit in a world of doubt,

bread is bro - ken, the wine is poured, Christ is spo - ken and seen and heard.
teach-ing peo - ple to live to bless, love in word and in deed ex - press.
gives us love to tell, bread to share: God (Im-man - u - el) ev - 'ry - where!

Refrain

Je-sus lives a-gain, earth can breathe a-gain, pass the Word a-round: loaves a-bound!

Text: Fred Kaan, b. 1929
Music: Jamaican folk tune, adapt. Doreen Potter, 1925–1980
© 1975 Hope Publishing Co.

LINSTEAD
L M and refrain

We All Are One in Mission

1 We all are one in mis - sion; we all are one in call,
2 We all are called to ser - vice, to wit - ness in God's name.
3 Now let us be u - nit - ed, and let our song be heard.

our var - ied gifts u - nit - ed by Christ, the Lord of all.
Our min - is - tries are dif - f'rent; our pur - pose is the same:
Now let us be a ves - sel for God's re - deem - ing Word.

A sin - gle great com - mis - sion com - pels us from a - bove
to touch the lives of oth - ers with God's sur - pris - ing grace,
We all are one in mis - sion; we all are one in call,

to plan and work to - geth - er that all may know Christ's love.
so ev - 'ry folk and na - tion may feel God's warm em - brace.
our var - ied gifts u - nit - ed by Christ, the Lord of all.

Text: Rusty Edwards, b. 1955
Music: Finnish folk tune, 19th cent.; arr. Joel Martinson
Text © 1986 Hope Publishing Co.
Arr. © 1992 Augsburg Fortress

KUORTANE
7 6 7 6 D

alt. tune: WEBB

756 Lord, You Give the Great Commission

1 Lord, you give the great com - mis - sion: "Heal the sick and
2 Lord, you call us to your ser - vice: "In my name bap -
3 Lord, you make the com - mon ho - ly: "This my bod - y,
4 Lord, you show us love's true mea - sure: "Fa - ther, what they
5 Lord, you bless with words as - sur - ing: "I am with you

preach the Word." Lest the Church ne - glect its mis - sion,
tize and teach." That the world may trust your prom - ise,
this my blood." Let us all, for earth's true glo - ry,
do, for - give." Yet we hoard as pri - vate trea - sure
to the end." Faith and hope and love re - stor - ing,

and the Gos - pel go un - heard, help us wit - ness
life a - bun - dant meant for each, give us all new
dai - ly lift life heav - en - ward, ask - ing that the
all that you so free - ly give. May your care and
may we serve as you in - tend and, a - mid the

to your pur - pose with re - newed in - teg - ri - ty.
fer - vor, draw us clos - er in com - mun - i - ty.
world a - round us share your chil - dren's lib - er - ty.
mer - cy lead us to a just so - ci - e - ty.
cares that claim us, hold in mind e - ter - ni - ty.

With the Spir - it's gifts em - pow'r us for the work of min - is - try.

Text: Jeffery Rowthorn, b. 1934
Music: Cyril V. Taylor, 1907–1991
Text © 1978 Hope Publishing Co.
Music © 1942, renewed 1970 Hope Publishing Co.

ABBOT'S LEIGH
8 7 8 7 D

STEWARDSHIP

Creating God, Your Fingers Trace 757

1 Cre - at - ing God, your fin - gers trace the bold de -
2 Sus - tain - ing God, your hands up - hold earth's mys - t'ries
3 Re - deem - ing God, your arms em - brace all now de -
4 In - dwell - ing God, your gos - pel claims one fam - 'ly

signs of far - thest space; let sun and moon and stars and
known or yet un - told; let wa - ter's fra - gile blend with
spised for creed or race; let peace, de - scend - ing like a
with a bil - lion names; let ev - 'ry life be touched by

light and what lies hid - den praise your might.
air, en - a - bling life, pro - claim your care.
dove, make known on earth your heal - ing love.
grace un - til we praise you face to face.

Text: Jeffery Rowthorn, b. 1934
Music: Vernon Griffiths, 1894–1985
Text © 1979 The Hymn Society of America, admin. Hope Publishing Co.
Music © 1971 Faber Music from *New Catholic Hymnal*

DUNEDIN
L M

758

Come to Us, Creative Spirit

1 Come to us, cre - a - tive Spir - it, in our
2 Po - et, paint - er, mu - sic - mak - er, all your
3 Word from God e - ter - nal spring - ing, fill our
4 In all plac - es and for - ev - er glo - ry

Fa - ther's house; ev - 'ry hu - man tal - ent hal - low,
trea - sures bring; crafts-man, ac - tor, grace-ful danc - er,
minds, we pray; and in all ar - tis - tic vi - sion
be ex - pressed to the Son, with God the Fa - ther

hid - den skills a - rouse, that with - in your earth - ly
make your of - fer - ing; join your hands in cel - e -
give in - teg - ri - ty: may the flame with - in us
and the Spir - it blessed: in our wor - ship and our

tem - ple, wise and sim - ple, may re - joice.
bra - tion: let cre - a - tion shout and sing!
burn - ing kin - dle yearn - ing day by day.
liv - ing keep us striv - ing for the best.

Text: David Mowbray, b. 1938
Tune: Richard Proulx, b. 1937
Text © 1979 Stainer and Bell Ltd. and Methodist Church Division of Education and Youth
Music © 1986 GIA Publications, Inc.

CASTLEWOOD
8 5 8 5 8 4 3

Accept, O Lord, the Gifts We Bring 759

1 Ac - cept, O Lord, the gifts we bring to place up - on your ta - ble.
2 The vines were plant - ed, seeds were sown. They grew in your good plea - sure.
3 Our hopes and dreams, our toils and cares we lift in pray'r be - fore you.

We do not wor - ship as we ought but on - ly as we're a - ble.
What once was com - mon, dai - ly food be - comes a ho - ly trea - sure.
Lord, by your grace now come to us, as hum - bly we a - dore you.

Text: Beth Bergeron Folkemer, b. 1957
Music: English folk tune, arr. Alice Parker, b. 1925
Text © 1990, arr. © 1995 Augsburg Fortress

BARBARA ALLEN
8 7 8 7

760   For the Fruit of All Creation

1 For the fruit of all cre - a - tion, thanks be to God.
2 In the just re - ward of la - bor, God's will is done.
3 For the har - vests of the Spir - it, thanks be to God.

For these gifts to ev - 'ry na - tion, thanks be to God.
In the help we give our neigh - bor, God's will is done.
For the good we all in - her - it, thanks be to God.

For the plow - ing, sow - ing, reap - ing, si - lent growth while we are sleep - ing,
In our world-wide task of car - ing for the hun - gry and de - spair - ing,
For the won - ders that as - tound us, for the truths that still con - found us,

fu - ture needs in earth's safe-keep - ing, thanks be to God.
in the har - vests we are shar - ing, God's will is done.
most of all, that love has found us, thanks be to God.

Text: Fred Pratt Green, b. 1903
Music: Welsh
Text © 1970 Hope Publishing Co.

AR HYD Y NOS
8 4 8 4 8 8 8 4

Now We Offer
Te ofrecemos

Now we of - fer you, our Fa - ther, with the bread and with the wine
Te o-fre - ce - mos, Pa - dre nues - tro, con el vi - no y con el pan,

all our joys and all our sor - rows all our strug-gles and our time.
nues-tras pe - nas y a - le - grí - as, el tra - ba - jo y nues-tro a - fán.

1 As the fields of wheat now grow - ing will be - come a ho - ly sign,
2 Like the grape put in the cel - lar, there to change in - to the wine,
3 In these gifts we see our one - ness through-out cit - y and the field,
4 All your peo - ple who are yearn-ing for the free - dom still a - head
5 We sing glo - ry to the Fa - ther and to Christ who lives a - bove,

so shall we re-veal you, Je - sus, that in us you now may shine.
all the poor on earth who suf - fer shed their sor - rows in this sign.
and we find a life of sol - ace where the scars of strife are healed.
of - fer fruits of your cre - a - tion in these gifts of wine and bread.
and we praise the Ho - ly Spir - it for the gift to us of love.

Text: *Misa popular nicaragüense*, tr. Gerald Thorson, b. 1921
Music: Nicaraguan folk tune, arr. Vernon Hamberg, b. 1948
Spanish text © Editorial Progreso, S.A. Mexico; tr. © 1989 Lutheran World Federation
Arr. © 1989 Augsburg Fortress

TE OFRECEMOS
8 7 8 7 and refrain

762

O Day of Peace

1 O day of peace that dim-ly shines through all our hopes and prayers and dreams,
2 Then shall the wolf dwell with the lamb; ne'er shall the fierce de - vour the small;

guide us to jus - tice, truth, and love, de-liv-ered from our self - ish schemes.
as beasts and cat - tle calm-ly graze, a lit - tle child shall lead them all.

May swords of hate fall from our hands, our hearts from en - vy find re-lease,
Then en - e - mies shall learn to love, all crea - tures find their true ac-cord;

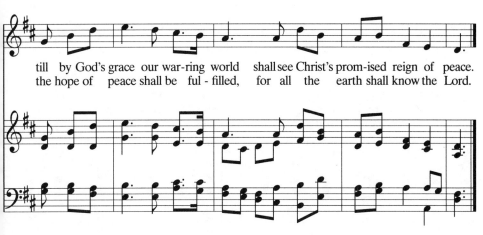

till by God's grace our war-ring world shall see Christ's prom-ised reign of peace.
the hope of peace shall be ful - filled, for all the earth shall know the Lord.

Text: Carl P. Daw, Jr., b. 1944
Music: C. Hubert H. Parry, 1848–1918
Text © 1982 Hope Publishing Co.

JERUSALEM
L M D

Let Justice Flow like Streams 763

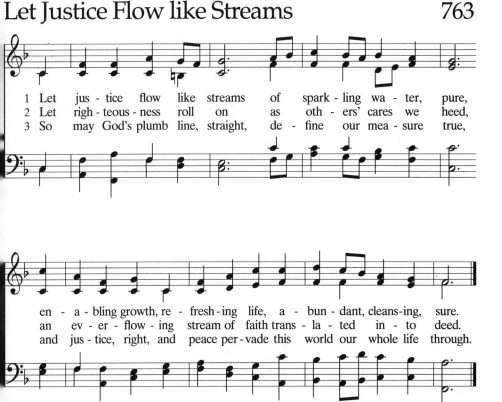

1 Let jus - tice flow like streams of spark - ling wa - ter, pure,
2 Let righ - teous - ness roll on as oth - ers' cares we heed,
3 So may God's plumb line, straight, de - fine our mea - sure true,

en - a - bling growth, re - fresh - ing life, a - bun - dant, cleans-ing, sure.
an ev - er - flow - ing stream of faith trans - la - ted in - to deed.
and jus - tice, right, and peace per - vade this world our whole life through.

Text: Jane Parker Huber, b. 1926
Music: Aaron Williams, 1731–1776
Text © 1984 Jane Parker Huber, admin. Westminster John Knox Press

ST. THOMAS
S M

764

Blest Are They

1 Blest are they, the poor in spir - it;
2 Blest are they, the low - ly ones; . . . .
3 Blest are they . . . . . who show mer - cy;
4 Blest are they . . . . . who seek peace; . . . .
5 Blest are you who suf - fer hate, ...

theirs is the king - dom of God.
they shall in - her - it the earth.
mer - cy shall . . . be theirs.
they are the chil - dren of God.
all . . . . be - cause . . . of me. Re -

Blest are they . . . . . full . . . . of sor - row; . . .
Blest are they who hun - ger and thirst; . . . . . .
Blest are they, the pure . . . . of heart . . . . . .
Blest are they who suf - fer in faith; the
joice, be glad, ... yours is the king - dom; . . .

they . . . . shall be con - soled.
they . . . . shall have their fill.
they . . . . . . shall see God!
glo - ry of God is theirs.
shine . . . . for all to see.

C   D^{sus}   D   C/G   G

Refrain

Re - joice and be glad!

C   D^{sus}   D   G   D/F#

Bless - ed are you,

Em   G/D   C   G/B

Hymn continues on next page.

Text: David Haas, b. 1957
Music: David Haas; arr. David Haas and Michael Joncas, b. 1951
© 1985 GIA Publications, Inc.

BLEST ARE THEY
irregular

Jesu, Jesu, Fill Us with Your Love 765

Je - su, Je - su, fill us with your love, show
us how to serve the neigh-bors we have from you.

1 Kneels at the feet of his friends, si - lent - ly wash - es their
2 Neigh-bors are wealth-y and poor, var - ied in col - or and
3 These are the ones we will serve, these are the ones we will
4 Kneel at the feet of our friends, si - lent - ly wash - ing their

feet, mas - ter who pours out him - self for them.
race, neigh-bors are near - by and far a - way.
love; all these are neigh-bors to us and you.
feet: this is the way we will live with you.

Text: Written for the Church in Ghana, Tom Colvin, b. 1925, alt.
Music: Ghanaian folk tune; adapt. Tom Colvin, b. 1925; arr. Jane Marshall, b. 1924
© 1969 and this arr. © 1982 Hope Publishing Co.

CHEREPONI
7 7 9 and refrain

766   We Come to the Hungry Feast

1 We come to the hun-gry feast hun-gry for a word of peace.
2 We come to the hun-gry feast hun-gry for a world re-leased
3 We come to the hun-gry feast hun-gry that the hun-ger cease,

To hun-gry hearts un - sat - is - fied the love of God is
from hun-gry folk of ev - 'ry kind, the poor in bod - y,
and know-ing, though we eat our fill, the hun - ger will stay

not de - nied.
poor in mind. We come, we come to the hun - gry feast.
with us still.

Text: Ray Makeever, b. 1943
Music: Ray Makeever, b. 1943
© Ray Makeever

HUNGRY FEAST
77889

All Things Bright and Beautiful 767

Refrain

All things bright and beau-ti-ful, all crea-tures great and small,

all things wise and won-der-ful, the Lord God made them all.

1 Each lit-tle flower that o - pens, each lit - tle bird that sings,
2 The pur-ple-head-ed moun-tains, the riv - er run-ning by,
3 The cold wind in the win - ter, the pleas-ant sum-mer sun,
4 God gave us eyes to see them, and lips that we might tell

Refrain

God made their glow-ing col - ors, God made their ti - ny wings.
the sun-set, and the morn - ing that bright-ens up the sky.
the ripe fruits in the gar - den, God made them ev - 'ry one.
how great is God Al - might - y, who has made all things well.

Text: Cecil F. Alexander, 1818–1895, alt.
Music: English tune, 17th cent., adapt. Martin Shaw, 1875–1958

ROYAL OAK
7 6 7 6 and refrain

768 He Comes to Us as One Unknown

1 He comes to us as one un-known, a breath un - seen, un -
2 He comes when souls in si - lence lie and thoughts of day de -
3 He comes to us in sound of seas, the o - cean's fume and
4 He comes in love as once he came by flesh and blood and
5 He comes in truth when faith is grown; be - lieved, o - beyed, a -

heard;   as though with-in a heart of stone, or shriv - eled seed in
part;   half - seen up - on the in - ward eye, a fall - ing star a -
foam;   yet small and still up - on the breeze, a wind that stirs the
birth;   to bear with-in our mor - tal frame a life, a death, a
dored;   the Christ in all the Scrip-tures shown, as yet un - seen, but

dark-ness sown, a pulse of be - ing stirred, a pulse of be - ing stirred.
cross the sky of night with-in the heart, of night with-in the heart.
tops of trees, a voice to call us home, a voice to call us home.
sav - ing name, for ev - 'ry child of earth, for ev - 'ry child of earth.
not un - known, our Sav - ior and our Lord, our Sav - ior and our Lord.

Text: Timothy Dudley-Smith, b. 1926
Music: C. Hubert H. Parry, 1848–1918
Text © 1973 Hope Publishing Co.

REPTON
868866

Mothering God, You Gave Me Birth 769

1 Moth - er - ing God, you gave me birth
2 Moth - er - ing Christ, you took my form,
3 Moth - er - ing Spir - it, nur - t'ring one,

in the bright morn - ing of this world.
of - fer - ing me your food of light,
in arms of pa - tience hold me close,

Cre - a - tor, source of ev - 'ry breath,
grain of new life, and grape of love,
so that in faith I root and grow

you are my rain, my wind, my sun.
your ver - y bod - y for my peace.
un - til I flow'r, un - til I know.

Text: Jean Janzen, b. 1933, based on Julian of Norwich, c. 1342- c. 1413
Music: Carolyn Jennings, b. 1936
Text © 1991 Jean Janzen.
Music © 1995 Augsburg Fortress.

NORWICH
L M

770 I Was There to Hear Your Borning Cry

1 "I was there to hear your born-ing cry, I'll be there when you are
2 "When you heard the won-der of the Word I was there to cheer you
3 "In the mid - dle a - ges of your life, not too old, no lon - ger

old. I re - joiced the day you were bap - tized to
on; you were raised to praise the liv - ing Lord, to
young, I'll be there to guide you through the night, com -

see your life un - fold. I was there when you were but a
whom you now be - long. If you find some-one to share your
plete what I've be - gun. When the eve - ning gent-ly clos - es

child, with a faith to suit you well;
time and you join your hearts as one,
in and you shut your wea - ry eyes,

in a blaze of light you wan - dered off to
I'll be there to make your vers - es rhyme from
I'll be there as I have al - ways been with

find where de - mons dwell."
dusk till ris - ing sun."
just one more sur - prise." 4 "I was there to hear your

born - ing cry, I'll be there when you are old. I re -

joiced the day you were bap-tized, to see your life un - fold."

Text: John Ylvisaker, b. 1937
Music: John Ylvisaker, b. 1937
© 1985 John Ylvisaker

WATERLIFE
9796D

771 Great Is Thy Faithfulness

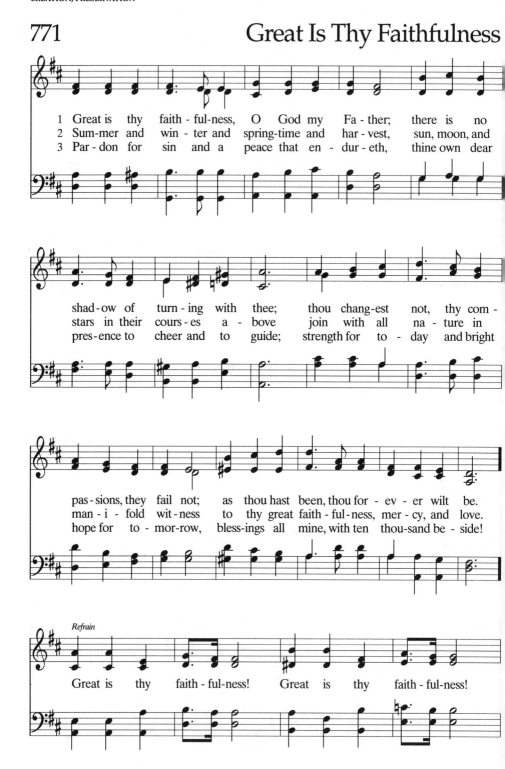

1 Great is thy faith - ful-ness, O God my Fa - ther; there is no
2 Sum-mer and win - ter and spring-time and har - vest, sun, moon, and
3 Par - don for sin and a peace that en - dur - eth, thine own dear

shad - ow of turn - ing with thee; thou chang-est not, thy com -
stars in their cours - es a - bove join with all na - ture in
pres - ence to cheer and to guide; strength for to - day and bright

pas - sions, they fail not; as thou hast been, thou for - ev - er wilt be.
man - i - fold wit - ness to thy great faith - ful-ness, mer - cy, and love.
hope for to - mor-row, bless-ings all mine, with ten thou-sand be - side!

Refrain

Great is thy faith - ful-ness! Great is thy faith - ful-ness!

Morn-ing by morn-ing new mer-cies I see; all I have need-ed thy hand hath pro - vid - ed; great is thy faith - ful-ness, Lord, un - to me!

Text: Thomas O. Chisholm, 1866–1960
Music: William M. Runyan, 1870–1957
© 1923, renewed 1951 Hope Publishing Co.

FAITHFULNESS
11 10 11 10 and refrain

PRAYER

O Lord, Hear My Prayer

The Lord Is My Song

772

O Lord, hear my prayer, O Lord, hear my prayer: when I call an - swer me.
The Lord is my song, the Lord is my praise: all my hope comes from God.

O Lord, hear my prayer, O Lord, hear my prayer, come and lis - ten to me.
The Lord is my song, the Lord is my praise: God, the well-spring of life.

Text: Psalm 102:1–2; adapt. Taizé Community, 1982
Music: Jacques Berthier, 1923–1994
© 1982, 1991 Les Presses de Taizé, admin. GIA Publications, Inc.

HEAR MY PRAYER
556 D

Send Me, Jesus
Thuma mina

1 Send me, Lord.

1 Send me, Je - sus, send me, Je - sus, send me,
Je - sus, lead me, Je - sus, lead me,
Je - sus, fill me, Je - sus, fill me,

2 Lead me, Lord.
3 Fill me, Lord.

Je - sus, send me, Lord. 2 Lead me,
Je - sus, lead me, Lord. 3 Fill me,
Je - sus, fill me, Lord.

1 Thuma mina
Thuma mina, thuma mina
Thuma mina, somandla

2 Roma nna
roma nna, roma nna
roma nna, modimo

Text: South African
Music: South African
© 1984 Utryck, admin. Walton Music Corp.

THUMA MINA
irregular

Dona Nobis Pacem

774

Do-na no-bis pa - cem, pa-cem. Do - na no - bis pa - cem.

Do - na no - bis pa-cem. Do-na no-bis pa - cem.

Do - na no - bis pa-cem. Do-na no-bis pa - cem.

Latin pronunciation: Dō-nȧ nō-bēs pȧ-chĕm (Give us peace)

Text: Traditional
Music: Traditional

DONA NOBIS PACEM
irregular

Lord, Listen to Your Children Praying

775

Lord, lis-ten to your chil-dren pray-ing,   Lord, send your Spir-it in this place;

Lord, lis-ten to your chil-dren pray-ing, send us love, send us pow'r, send us grace.

Text: Ken Medema, b.1943
Music: Ken Medema, b. 1943
© 1973 Hope Publishing Co.

CHILDREN PRAYING
irregular

776

Be Thou My Vision

1 Be thou my vi - sion, O Lord of my heart;
2 Be thou my wis - dom, and thou my true word;
3 Rich - es I heed not, nor vain, emp - ty praise,
4 Light of my soul, af - ter vic - to - ry won,

naught be all else to me, save that thou art:
I ev - er with thee and thou with me, Lord.
thou mine in - her - i - tance, now and al - ways:
may I reach heav - en's joys, O heav - en's Sun!

thou my best thought . . . by day and by night,
Thou my soul's shel - ter, thou my high tower,
thou, and thou on - ly, first in my heart,
Heart of my own heart, what - ev - er be - fall,

wak - ing or sleep - ing, thy pres - ence my light.
raise thou me heav'n - ward, O Pow'r of my pow'r.
great God of heav - en, my trea - sure thou art.
still be my vi - sion, O Rul - er of all.

Text: Irish 8th–10th cent.; tr. Mary E. Byrne, 1880–1931; vers. Eleanor H. Hull, 1860–1935, alt.
Music: Irish tune

SLANE
10 10 9 10

In the Morning When I Rise
Give Me Jesus

777

1 In the morn-ing when I rise, in the morn-ing when I rise,
2 Dark . . . mid-night was my cry, dark . . . mid-night was my cry,
3 Just a-bout the break of day, just a-bout the break of day,
4 Oh, . . . when I come to die, oh, . . . when I come to die,
5 And . . . when I want to sing, and . . . when I want to sing,

in the morn-ing when I rise, give me Je - sus.
dark . . . mid-night was my cry, give me Je - sus.
just a-bout the break of day, give me Je - sus.
oh, . . . when I come to die, give me Je - sus.
and . . . when I want to sing, give me Je - sus.

Refrain

Give me Je - sus, give me Je - sus.

You may have all the rest, give me Je - sus.

Text: African American spiritual
Music: African American spiritual, arr. L.L. Fleming, b. 1936
Arr. © 1973 Augsburg Publishing House

GIVE ME JESUS
7 7 7 4 and refrain

778

O Christ the Same

1 O Christ the same, through all our sto - ry's pag - es—
2 O Christ the same, the friend of sin - ners, shar - ing
3 O Christ the same, se - cure with - in whose keep - ing

our loves and hopes, our fail - ures and our fears;
our in - most thoughts, the se - crets none can hide;
our lives and loves, our days and years re - main;

e - ter - nal Lord, the king of all the a - ges,
still as of old up - on your bod - y bear - ing
our work and rest, our wak - ing and our sleep - ing,

un - chang - ing still a - mid the pass - ing years:
the marks of love in tri - umph glo - ri - fied:
our calm and storm, our plea - sure and our pain:

O liv - ing Word, the source of all cre - a - tion,
O Son of Man, who stooped for us from heav - en—
O Lord of love, for all our joys and sor - rows,

who spread the skies and set the stars a - blaze;
O Prince of life, in all your sav - ing power;
for all our hopes when earth shall fade and flee;

O Christ the same, who wrought our whole sal - va - tion,
O Christ the same, to whom our hearts are giv - en:
O Christ the same, be - yond our brief to - mor - rows,

we bring our thanks for all our yes - ter - days.
we bring our thanks for this the pres - ent hour.
we bring our thanks for all that is to be.

Text: Timothy Dudley-Smith, b. 1926
Music: Irish tune, arr. John Barnard, b. 1948
Text © 1984 and arr. © 1982 Hope Publishing Co.

LONDONDERRY AIR
11 10 11 10 D

You Who Dwell in the Shelter of the Lord

779

On Eagle's Wings

1 You who . . . dwell in the shel - ter of the Lord, who a -
2 Snares of the fowl - er will nev - er cap - ture you, and
3 For to the an - gels God's giv - en a com - mand to

bide in this shad-ow for life, say to the Lord: "My . . .
fam - ine will bring you no fear, un - der God's wings your . . .
guard you in all of your ways; up - on their hands they will

ref - uge, . . . my . . . rock . . . . in whom I . . . trust!"
ref - uge . . . with . . . faith - ful - ness . . . . . . your . . . shield.
bear you up, lest you dash . . . . your foot a - gainst a stone.

Text: Michael Joncas, b. 1951
Music: Michael Joncas, b. 1951

ON EAGLE'S WINGS
irregular

What a Fellowship, What a Joy Divine

Leaning on the Everlasting Arms

780

1 What a fel-low-ship, what a joy di-vine,
2 Oh, how sweet to walk in this pil-grim way, lean-ing on the ev-er-last-ing arms;
3 What have I to dread, what have I to fear,

what a bless-ed-ness, what a peace is mine,
oh, how bright the path grows from day to day, lean-ing on the ev-er-last-ing arms.
I have bless-ed peace with my Lord so near,

Refrain

Lean - ing, lean - ing, safe and se-cure from all a-larms;

Lean-ing on Je - sus, lean-ing on Je - sus,

lean - ing, lean - ing, lean-ing on the ev-er-last-ing arms.

lean-ing on Je - sus, lean-ing on Je - sus,

Text: Elisha Hoffman, 1839–1929
Music: Anthony J. Showalter, 1858–1924

SHOWALTER
10 9 10 9 and refrain

My Life Flows On in Endless Song   781

1 My   life flows on   in   end-less song; a-bove earth's lam-en-ta - tion,
2 Through all   the tu - mult   and the strife, I   hear that   mu-sic ring-ing.
3 What   though my joys   and   com-forts die? The Lord my   Sav-ior liv-eth.
4 The   peace of Christ makes fresh my heart, a   foun-tain   ev - er spring-ing!

I   catch the sweet, though far-off   hymn   that hails a   new cre-a - tion.
It   finds   an ech - o   in my   soul.   How can I   keep from sing-ing?
What though the dark - ness gath-er   round? Songs in   the night he   giv-eth.
All   things are mine since   I   am   his!   How can I   keep from sing-ing?

Refrain

No   storm can shake my   in-most calm   while to   that Rock I'm   cling-ing.

Since Christ is   Lord of   heav-en and earth,   how can I keep   from sing-ing?

Text: Robert Lowry, 1826–1899
Music: Robert Lowry, 1826–1899, alt.

HOW CAN I KEEP FROM SINGING
8 7 8 7 and refrain

782 All My Hope on God Is Founded

1 All my hope on God is found - ed who will all my
2 Mor - tal pride and earth - ly glo - ry, sword and crown be -
3 Great thy good - ness e'er en - dur - ing; deep thy wis - dom,
4 Still from earth to God e - ter - nal sac - ri - fice of

trust re - new, who through change and chance will guide me,
tray our trust; what with care and toil we fash - ion,
pass - ing thought; splen - dor, light and life at - tend thee,
praise be done, high a - bove all prais - es prais - ing

on - ly good and on - ly true. God un - known, from thy
tow'r and tem - ple, fall to dust. But thy pow'r, hour by
beau - ty spring - ing out of nought. Ev - er - more from God's
for the gift of God's own Son. Christ shall call one and

throne call my heart to be thine own.
hour, is my tem - ple and my tow'r.
store new - born worlds rise and a - dore.
all: you that fol - low shall not fall.

Text: Joachim Neander, 1650–1680; para. Robert Bridges, 1844–1930, alt.
Music: Herbert Howells, 1892–1983
Music © Novello & Co., Ltd.

MICHAEL
8 7 8 7 3 3 7

Seek Ye First the Kingdom of God

783

Descant

Al - le - lu - ia, al -
le - lu - ia, al - le -
lu - ia, al - le - lu - ia.

1 Seek ye ... first the king - dom of God and its
2 Ask and it shall be giv - en un - to you; seek and
3 We do not live by bread ... a - lone, but by

righ - teous - ness, and all these things shall be
you shall find; knock and the door shall be
ev - 'ry word that pro - ceeds from the

add - ed un - to you. Al - le - lu, al - le - lu - ia.
o - pened un - to you. Al - le - lu, al - le - lu - ia.
mouth .. of ... God. Al - le - lu, al - le - lu - ia.

Text: st. 1, Matt. 6:33, adapt. Karen Lafferty, b. 1948; st. 2, Matt. 7:7; st. 3, Matt. 4:4
Music: Karen Lafferty, b. 1948
Text st. 1 and music © 1972 Maranatha! Music, admin. The Copyright Co.

LAFFERTY
irregular

You Have Come Down to the Lakeshore

784

Tú has venido a la orilla

1 You have come down to the lake - shore seek - ing
2 You know full well what I have, Lord: nei - ther
3 You need my hands, my ex - haus - tion, work - ing
4 You who have fished oth-er wa - ters; you, the

nei - ther the wise nor the wealth - y, but on - ly
trea - sure nor wea-pons for con - quest, just these my
love for the rest of the wea - ry— a love that's
long - ing of souls that are yearn - ing: O lov - ing

ask - ing for me to fol - low.
fish nets and will for work - ing.
will - ing to go on lov - ing.
Friend, you have come to call me.

Refrain (Estribillo)

Sweet Lord, you have looked in - to my eyes;
Se - ñor: me has mi - ra - do_a los o - jos;

kind-ly smil - ing, you've called out my name.
son - ri - en - do, has di - cho mi nom - bre;

On the sand I have a - ban-doned my small boat;
en la_a - re - na he de - ja - do mi bar - ca;

now with you, I will seek oth - er seas.
jun - to_a ti bus - ca - ré o - tro mar.

1 *Tú has venido_a la_orilla;*
  no_has buscado ni_a sabios, ni_a ricos;
  tan sólo quieres que yo te siga. Estribillo

2 *Tú sabes bien lo que tengo:*
  en mi barca no_hay oro no_espadas;
  tan sólo redes y mi trabajo. Estribillo

3 *Tú necesitas mis manos,*
  mi cansancio que_a otros descanse,
  amor que quiera sequir amando. Estribillo

4 *Tú, Pescador de_otros mares,*
  ansia_eterna de_almas que_esperan.
  Amigo bueno, que_así me llamas. Estribillo

Text: Cesáreo Gabaraín, 1936–1991; tr. Madeleine Forell Marshall, b. 1946
Music: Cesáreo Gabaraín, 1936–1991
Spanish text and music © 1979 Ediciones Paulinas, admin. OCP Publications
Tr. © Editorial Avance Luterano

PESCADOR DE HOMBRES
8 10 10 and refrain

785   Weary of All Trumpeting

1 Wea-ry of all trum-pet-ing, wea-ry of all kill-ing,
  wea-ry of all songs that sing prom-ise, non-ful-fill-ing,
  we would raise, O Christ, one song: we would join in sing-ing
  that great mu-sic pure and strong, where-with heav'n is ring-ing.

2 Cap-tain Christ, O low-ly Lord, Ser-vant King, your dy-ing
  bade us sheathe the fool-ish sword, bade us cease de-ny-ing.
  Trum-pet with your Spir-it's breath through each height and hol-low;
  in-to your self-giv-ing death, call us all to fol-low.

3 To the tri-umph of your cross sum-mon all the liv-ing;
  sum-mon us to live by loss, gain-ing all by giv-ing.
  Suff'r-ing all, that all may see tri-umph in sur-ren-der;
  leav-ing all, that we may be part-ners in your splen-dor.

Text: Martin Franzmann, 1907–1976
Music: Hugo Distler, 1908–1942, arr. Jan Bender, 1909–1994
© 1972 Chantry Music Press

DISTLER
7 6 7 6 D

Amen, We Praise Your Name
Amen, siakudumisa

Leader

Sing prais - es!
Ma - si thi!

Sing prais - es!
Ma - si thi!

Congregation

A-men, we praise your name, O God!
A - men, si - a - ku - du - mi - sa!

Sing prais - es!
Ma - si thi!

A-men, we praise your name, O God!
A - men, si - a - ku - du - mi - sa!

A-men, a - men.
A - men, ba - wo.

A-men, a - men.
A - men, ba - wo.

A-men, we praise your name, O God!
A - men, si - a - ku - du - mi - sa!

Sing prais - es!
Ma - si thi!

Text: South African traditional
Music: attr. S.C. Molefe; as taught by Gobingca Mxadana
Music © Gobingca Mxadana

AMEN SIAKUDUMISA
irregular

787 Glory to God, We Give You Thanks

1 Glo - ry to God, we give you thanks and praise;
2 Lord Je - sus Christ, the Fa - ther's on - ly Son,
3 A - lone, O Christ, you on - ly are the Lord,

of heav'n - ly joy and earth - ly peace we sing.
you bore for us the load of this world's sin.
at God's right hand in maj - es - ty most high:

We wor - ship you, to you our hearts we raise,
O Lamb of God, your glo - rious vic - t'ry won,
who, with the Spir - it wor - shiped and a - dored,

Lord God, al - might - y Fa - ther, heav'n - ly King.
re - ceive our pray'r, grant us your peace with - in.
with all the heav'n - ly host we glo - ri - fy.

Text: Edwin LeGrice, based on *Gloria in excelsis Deo*
Music: Walter Greatorex, 1877–1949
Text © 1991 Kevin Mayhew Ltd., Lic. #499082
Music © Oxford University Press

WOODLANDS
10 10 10 10

Glory to God, Glory in the Highest 788

Leader
Glo-ry to God, glo-ry to God, glo-ry in the high - est!

All
Glo-ry to God, glo-ry to God, glo-ry in the high - est!

Leader
To God be glo-ry for-ev - er!

All
To God be glo-ry for-ev - er!

Leader
Al-le-lu-ia! A-men!

Leader
Al-le-lu-ia! A-men!

Group 1
Al-le-lu-ia! A-men! Al-le-lu-ia! A-men!

Group 1, 2
Al-le-lu-ia! A-men!

Leader
Al-le-lu-ia! A-men!

Group 1, 2, 3
Al-le-lu-ia! A-men! Al-le-lu-ia! A-men! Al-le-lu-ia! A-men! Al-le-lu-ia! A - men!

Text: Traditional
Music: Peruvian traditional

GLORIA PERU
irregular

789 Now the Feast and Celebration

Refrain

Now the feast and cel - e - bra - tion, all of cre - a - tion

sings for joy to the God of life and love and free-dom;

praise and glo - ry for - ev - er - more!

Stanza 1

1 Now is the feast of the Lamb once slain,

whose blood has freed and u - nit - ed us

Text: Marty Haugen, b. 1950
Music: Marty Haugen, b. 1950
© 1990 GIA Publications, Inc.

NOW THE FEAST
irregular

Praise to You, O God of Mercy
Thanks Be to You

1 Praise to you, O God of mer-cy! Thanks be to you for -
2 From of old you loved and sought us! Thanks be to you for -
3 Praise to you, O God of mer-cy! Thanks be to you for -

ev - er! Rais - ing high the weak and low - ly:
ev - er! Truth and jus - tice you have taught us:
ev - er! Rais - ing high the weak and low - ly:

3rd time to Coda

thanks be to you for - ev - er!
thanks be to you for - ev - er!
thanks be to you for - ev - er!

Text: Marty Haugen, b. 1950
Music: Marty Haugen, b. 1950
© 1990 GIA Publications, Inc.

THANKS BE TO YOU
irregular

791 Alabaré

Alabaré a mi Señor: I will praise my Lord.

Thou - sands were pray - ing, ten thou-sands re - joic - ing, and
Pow - er and rich - es, and wis - dom and strength . . . and
Bless - ing and hon - or and glo - ry and might . . . to

Refrain

all were sing - ing prais - es to the Lord.
hon - or and all bless - ing shall be his.
God and to the Lamb be with - out end.

Text: Manuel José Alonso and José Pagán; English text composite
Music: Manuel José Alonso, José Pagán
Spanish text and music © 1979 Manuel José Alonso, José Pagán, and Ediciones Musical PAX, admin. OCP Publications

ALABARÉ
irregular

Amen, Hallelujah 792

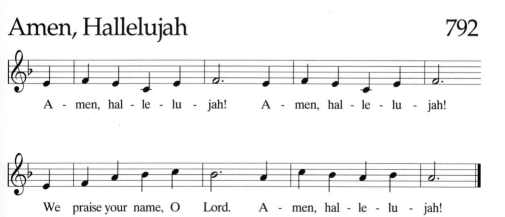

A - men, hal - le - lu - jah! A - men, hal - le - lu - jah!

We praise your name, O Lord. A - men, hal - le - lu - jah!

Text: Traditional
Music: Javanese tune, arr. Sutarno

AMIN HALELUYA
irregular

793 Shout for Joy Loud and Long

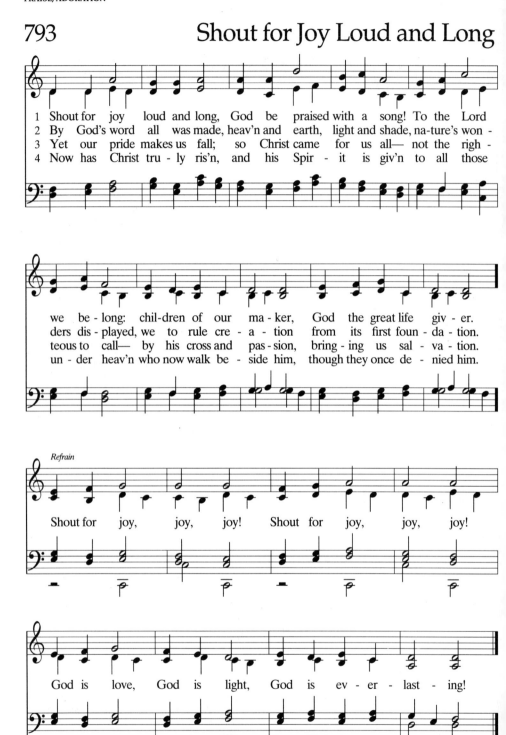

1 Shout for joy loud and long, God be praised with a song! To the Lord
2 By God's word all was made, heav'n and earth, light and shade, na-ture's won -
3 Yet our pride makes us fall; so Christ came for us all— not the righ -
4 Now has Christ tru - ly ris'n, and his Spir - it is giv'n to all those

we be - long: chil-dren of our ma - ker, God the great life giv - er.
ders dis - played, we to rule cre - a - tion from its first foun - da - tion.
teous to call— by his cross and pas - sion, bring - ing us sal - va - tion.
un - der heav'n who now walk be - side him, though they once de - nied him.

Refrain

Shout for joy, joy, joy! Shout for joy, joy, joy!

God is love, God is light, God is ev - er - last - ing!

Text: David Mowbray, b. 1938
Music: *Piae cantiones*, 1582; arr. Paul Manz, b. 1919
Text © 1982 Hope Publishing Co.
Arr. © 1995 Augsburg Fortress

PERSONENT HODIE
6 6 6 6 6 and refrain

Many and Great, O God, Are Your Works 794

1 Man - y and great, O God, are your works,
2 Grant un - to us com - mu - nion with you,

Mak - er of earth and sky. Your hands have
O Star - a - bid - ing One. Come un - to

set the heav'ns with stars; your fin - gers spread the
us and dwell with us; with you are found the

hills and plains. Lo, your word formed the
gifts of life. Bless us with life that

wa - ters deep; o - ceans o - bey your voice.
has no end, e - ter - nal life with you.

Text: Joseph R. Renville,1779–1846, para. Philip Frazier, 1892–1964, alt.
Music: Dakota tune; arr. *Songs of the People*, 1986
Arr. © 1986 Augsburg Publishing House

LAC QUI PARLE
968886

Oh, Sing to the Lord
Cantad al Señor

795

1 Oh, sing to the Lord, oh, sing God a new song.
2 For God is the Lord, and God has done won - ders.
3 So dance for our God and blow all the trum - pets.
4 Oh, shout to our God, who gave us the Spir - it.
5 For Je - sus is Lord! A - men! Al - le - lu - ia!

Oh, sing to the Lord, oh, sing God a new song.
For God is the Lord, and God has done won - ders.
So dance for our God and blow all the trum - pets.
Oh, shout to our God, who gave us the Spir - it.
For Je - sus is Lord! A - men! Al - le - lu - ia!

Oh, sing to the Lord, oh, sing God a new song.
For God is the Lord, and God has done won - ders.
So dance for our God and blow all the trum - pets,
Oh, shout to our God, who gave us the Spir - it.
For Je - sus is Lord! A - men! Al - le - lu - ia!

Oh, sing to our God, oh, sing to our God.
Oh, sing to our God, oh, sing to our God.
and sing to our God, and sing to our God.
Oh, sing to our God, oh, sing to our God.
Oh, sing to our God, oh, sing to our God.

1 Cantad al Señor un cántico nuevo.
Cantad al Señor un cántico nuevo.
Cantad al Señor un cántico nuevo.
¡cantad al Señor, cantad al Señor!

2 Porque el Señor ha hecho prodigios.
Porque el Señor ha hecho prodigios,
Porque el Señor ha hecho prodigios,
¡cantad al Señor, cantad al Señor!

3 Cantad al Señor, alabadle con arpa.
Cantad al Señor, alabadle con arpa,
Cantad al Señor, alabadle con arpa,
¡cantad al Señor, cantad al Señor!

4 Es él que nos da el Espíritu Santo.
Es él que nos da el Espíritu Santo,
Es él que nos da el Espíritu Santo,
¡cantad al Señor, cantad al Señor!

5 ¡Jesus es Señor! ¡Amén, aleluya!
¡Jesus es Señor! ¡Amén, aleluya!
¡Jesus es Señor! ¡Amén, aleluya!
¡cantad al Señor, cantad al Señor!

Text: Brazilian folk song; tr. Gerhard Cartford, b. 1923
Music: Brazilian folk tune; arr. Gerhard Cartford, b. 1923
Tr. & arr. © Gerhard Cartford

CANTAD AL SEÑOR
56565655

My Lord of Light 796

1 My Lord of light who made the worlds, in   wis - dom you have   spo - ken;
2 My Lord of love who knew no sin,   a   sin - ner's death en - dur - ing:
3 My Lord of life who came in fire   when Christ was high as - cend - ed:
4 My Lord of lords, one Trin - i - ty,   to   your pure name be   giv - en

but those who heard your wise com-mands your ho - ly law have bro - ken.
for   us you wore a   crown of thorns, a crown of life se - cur - ing.
your burn-ing love is   now re - leased, our days of fear are   end - ed.
all   glo - ry now and ev - er - more, all praise in earth and   heav - en.

Text: Christopher Idle, b. 1938
Music: English folk tune, arr. Alice Parker, b. 1925
Text © 1982 Hope Publishing Co.
Arr. © 1995 Augsburg Fortress

BARBARA ALLEN
8787

797

O God beyond All Praising

1 O God be-yond all prais-ing, we wor-ship you to - day
2 Then hear, O gra-cious Sav - ior, ac - cept the love we bring,

and sing the love a - maz-ing that songs can-not re - pay;
that we who know your fa - vor may serve you as our king;

for we can on - ly won - der at ev - 'ry gift you send,
and wheth - er our to - mor - rows be fill'd with good or ill,

at bless-ings with - out num - ber and mer-cies with - out end:
we'll tri - umph through our sor - rows and rise to bless you still:

we lift our hearts be-fore you and wait up-on your Word,
to mar-vel at your beau-ty and glo-ry in your ways,

we hon-or and a-dore you, our great and might-y Lord.
and make a joy-ful du-ty our sac-ri-fice of praise.

Text: Michael Perry, b. 1942
Music: Gustav Holst, 1874–1934
Text © 1982 Hope Publishing Co.

THAXTED
13 13 13 13 13 13

Bless the Lord, O My Soul   798

Bless the Lord, O my soul; bless the Lord, O my soul;

and all that is with-in me bless God's ho-ly name.

Text: Ps. 103:1
Music: Traditional

PRAISE PSALM 103
irregular

When Long Before Time

The Singer and the Song

1 When long be-fore time and the worlds were be-gun,
2 The si-lence was bro-ken when God sang the Song,
3 The sounds of the crea-tures were one with their Lord's,
4 Though down through the a-ges the Song dis-ap-peared,

when there was no earth and no sky and no sun,
and light pierced the dark-ness and rhy-thm be-gan,
their har-mo-nies sweet and be-fit-ting the Word;
its har-mo-nies bro-ken and al-most un-heard,

and all was deep si-lence and night reigned su-preme,
and with its first birth-cries cre-a-tion was born,
the Sing-er was pleased as the earth sang the Song,
the Sing-er comes to us to sing it a-gain,

and e-ven our Mak-er had on-ly a dream—
and crea-ture-ly voic-es sang praise to the morn.
the choir of the crea-tures re-ech-oed it long.
our God-is-with-us in the world now as then.

5 The Light has returned as it came once before,
   the Song of the Lord is our own song once more,
   so let us all sing with one heart and one voice
   the Song of the Singer in whom we rejoice.

6 To you, God the Singer, our voices we raise,
   to you, Song Incarnate, we give all our praise,
   to you, Holy Spirit, our life and our breath,
   be glory for ever, through life and through death.

Text: Peter W. A. Davison, b. 1936
Music: Peter W. A. Davison, b. 1936; arr. George Black
Text and tune © Peter W. A. Davison
Arr. © George Black

THE SINGER AND THE SONG
11 11 11 11

Each Morning Brings Us   800

1 Each morn - ing brings us fresh out - poured the lov - ing kind-ness
2 O God, the star of dawn-ing day, give us that light for
3 Walk with us in the light of day, that we may ev - er,

of the Lord. It ends not as the day goes
which we pray. Your ho - ly flame with - in us
come what may, in hope en - dure, in faith be

past, but gives us strength while life shall last.
glow, that we no lack of grace may know.
strong; a - bide in us our whole life long.

Text: Johannes Zwick, 1496–1542, tr. Margaret Barclay, alt.
Music: Johann Walter, 1496–1570

ALL MORGEN IST GANZ FRISCH
L M

801 Thine the Amen, Thine the Praise

1 Thine the a - men thine the praise al - le - lu - ias an - gels raise
2 Thine the life e - ter - nal - ly thine the prom - ise let there be
3 Thine the tru - ly thine the yes thine the ta - ble we the guest
4 Thine the king - dom thine the prize thine the won - der full sur - prise
5 Thine the glo - ry in the night no more dy - ing on - ly light

thine the ev - er - last - ing head thine the break - ing of the bread
thine the vi - sion thine the tree all the earth on bend - ed knee
thine the mer - cy all from thee thine the glo - ry yet to be
thine the ban - quet then the praise then the jus - tice of thy ways
thine the riv - er thine the tree then the Lamb e - ter - nal - ly

thine the glo - ry thine the sto - ry thine the har - vest then the cup
gone the nail - ing gone the rail - ing gone the plead - ing gone the cry
then the ring - ing and the sing - ing then the end of all the war
thine the glo - ry thine the sto - ry then the wel - come to the least
then the ho - ly ho - ly ho - ly cel - e - bra - tion ju - bi - lee

thine the vine - yard then the cup is lift - ed up lift - ed up.
gone the sigh - ing gone the dy - ing what was loss lift - ed high.
thine the liv - ing thine the lov - ing ev - er - more ev - er - more.
then the won - der all in - creas - ing at thy feast at thy feast.
thine the splen - dor thine the bright - ness on - ly thee on - ly thee.

Text: Herbert F. Brokering, b. 1926
Music: Carl Schalk, b. 1929
© 1983 Augsburg Publishing House

THINE
14 14 15 14

When in Our Music God Is Glorified 802

1 When in our mu - sic God is glo - ri - fied,
2 How of - ten, mak - ing mu - sic, we have found
3 So has the Church in lit - ur - gy and song,
4 And did not Je - sus sing a psalm that night
5 Let ev - 'ry in - stru-ment be tuned for praise!

and ad - o - ra - tion leaves no room for pride,
a new di - men - sion in the world of sound,
in faith and love, through cen - tu - ries of wrong,
when ut - most e - vil strove a - gainst the light?
Let all re - joice who have a voice to raise!

it is as though the whole cre - a - tion cried
as wor - ship moved us to a more pro - found
borne wit - ness to the truth in ev - 'ry tongue,
Then let us sing, for whom he won the fight:
And may God give us faith to sing al - ways

1-4
Al - le - lu - ia!

5
Al - le - lu - ia!

Text: Fred Pratt Green, b. 1903
Music: Charles V. Stanford, 1852–1924
Text © 1972 Hope Publishing Co.

ENGELBERG
10 10 10 4

Acknowledgments

The liturgical material on pages 5-53 is covered by the copyright of this book.

Material from the following sources is acknowledged:

Lutheran Book of Worship and *Lutheran Book of Worship Ministers Edition*, ©1978 Lutheran Church in America, The American Lutheran Church, The Evangelical Lutheran Church of Canada, and The Lutheran Church-Missouri Synod.

Occasional Services, © 1982 Association of Evangelical Lutheran Churches, Lutheran Church in America, The American Lutheran Church, and The Evangelical Lutheran Church of Canada.

Book of Common Prayer (1979) of The Episcopal Church.

Prayers We Have in Common, © 1975 International Consultation on English Texts: the Apostles' and Nicene Creeds.

Praying Together, © 1988 English Language Liturgical Consultation: the Apostles' Creed, the Nicene Creed, the preface dialogue, the canticle texts "Lord, have mercy," "Glory to God in the highest," "Holy, holy, holy Lord," "Lamb of God," and "Now, Lord, you let your servant go in peace."

The Revised Common Lectionary, © 1992 Consultation on Common Texts.

New Revised Standard Version of the Bible, © 1989, Division of Christian Education of the National Council of Churches of Christ in the United States of America.

Composers of liturgical music are acknowledged: Daniel Kallman (b. 1956), Jeremy Young (b. 1948), Robert Buckley Farlee (b. 1950), and J. Bert Carlson (b. 1937).

Authors/translators of liturgical texts are acknowledged: Susan Palo Cherwien (b. 1953), Gail Ramshaw (b. 1947), Martin A. Seltz (b. 1951), and Frank Stoldt (b. 1958).

ELCA churchwide and publishing house staff: Norma Aamodt-Nelson, Ruth Allin, Lorraine Brugh, Carol Carver, M. Alexandra George, Lynette Johnson, Mary Ann Moller-Gunderson, Mark Junkert, Ellen Maly, Paul R. Nelson, Kristine Oberg, Rachel Riensche, Michael Rothaar, Ann M. P. Schroeder, Martin A. Seltz (co-editor), Frank Stoldt (co-editor), Samuel Torvend, Karen Ward.

Music engraving: A-R Editions, Inc., Madison, WI.

Indexes: Craig Mueller, Paul Schuessler.

Proofreading: Lila M. Aamodt, Becky Brantner-Christianson, Robert A. Rimbo.

Copyright and Permissions

Copyright Holders and Administrators

ABINGDON PRESS (THE UNITED METHODIST PUBLISHING HOUSE)
201 Eighth Ave. S., P.O. Box 801
Nashville, TN 37202
615/749-6422   FAX 615/749-6512

ARCHDIOCESE OF PHILADELPHIA, Music Office
222 North 17th St.
Philadelphia, PA 19103-1299
215/587-3696   FAX 215/587-3561

ASIAN INSTITUTE FOR LITURGY AND MUSIC
P.O. Box 3167
Manila 2800, Philippines
                     011-632-721-6140
          FAX 011-632-722-1490

AUGSBURG FORTRESS
426 S. 5th Street, P.O. Box 1209
Minneapolis, MN 55440
800/328-4648   FAX 612/330-3455

CHURCH HYMNAL CORPORATION
445 Fifth Avenue
New York, NY 10016
800/233-6602   FAX 212/779-3392

CONSULTATION ON COMMON TEXTS/ENGLISH LANGUAGE LITURGICAL CONSULTATION
1275 K Street NW
Washington, DC 20005-4097
202/347-0800   FAX 202/347-1839

COPYRIGHT COMPANY
40 Music Square East
Nashville, TN 37203
615/244-5588   FAX 615/244-5591

CPH PUBLISHING
3558 South Jefferson Ave.
St. Louis, MO 63118
800/325-0191   FAX 314/268-1329

DAVID HIGHAM ASSOCIATES
5-8 Lower John Street, Golden Square
London W1R 4HA, England
                     011-44-71-437-7888
          FAX 011-44-71-437-1072

GIA PUBLICATIONS
7404 South Mason Avenue
Chicago, IL 60638
708/496-3800   FAX 708/496-2130

HAL LEONARD CORPORATION
7777 W. Bluemound Rd.
P.O. Box 13819
Milwaukee, WI 53213
414/774-3630   FAX 414/774-8387

HINSHAW MUSIC, INC.
P.O. Box 470
Chapel Hill, NC 27514
919/933-1691   FAX 919/967-3399

HOPE PUBLISHING COMPANY
380 South Main Place
Carol Stream, IL 60188
800/323-1049   FAX 708/665-2552

INTEGRITY MUSIC
1000 Cody Road
Mobile, AL 36695
205/633-9000   FAX 205/633-5202

KEVIN MAYHEW LTD.
Rattlesden, Bury St. Edwards
Suffolk, IP3 0SZ England
                     011-44-973-7978
          FAX 011-44-973-7834

LITURGICAL PRESS, THE
Box 7500, Collegeville, MN 56321
612/363-2213   FAX 612/363-3299

LUTHERAN THEOLOGICAL COLLEGE AT MAKUMIRA
Tanzania, East Africa
c/o Augsburg Fortress

MORNINGSTAR MUSIC
2117 59th Street
St. Louis, MO 63110
800/647-2117   FAX 314/647-2777

NEW DAWN MUSIC
P.O. Box 13248
Portland, OR 97213
800/243-3296   FAX 503/282-3486

NEW GENERATION PUBLISHERS
John Ylvisaker
Box 321, Waverly, IA 50677
319/352-4396

NOVELLO AND COMPANY
8/9 Frith Street
London W1V 5TZ, England
                     011-44-71-434-0066
          FAX 011-44-71-287-6329

OCP PUBLICATIONS
5536 NE Hassalo
Portland, OR 97213
800/547-8992   FAX 503/282-3486

OXFORD UNIVERSITY PRESS
200 Madison Ave.
New York, NY 10016
212/679-7300   FAX 212/725-2972

OXFORD UNIVERSITY PRESS
3 Park Road
London NW1 6XN, England
                     011-44-71-724-7484
          FAX 011-41-71-723-5033

PILGRIM PRESS/ UNITED CHURCH PRESS
700 Prospect Ave. E
Cleveland, OH 44115-1100
216/736-3700   FAX 216/736-3703

RESOURCE PUBLICATIONS
160 E. Virginia St. #290
San Jose, CA 95112-5876
408/286-8505   FAX 408/287-8748

SELAH PUBLISHING COMPANY
58 Pearl Street, P.O. Box 3037
Kingston, NY 12401-0902
914/338-2816   FAX 914/338-2991

SPARROW CORPORATION
P.O. Box 5010
Brentwood, TN 37024-5010
615/371-6997   FAX 615/371-6800

WALTON MUSIC CORPORATION
170 NE 33rd St., P.O. Box 24330
Fort Lauderdale, FL 33307
305/563-1844   FAX 305/563-9006

WESTMINSTER JOHN KNOX PRESS
100 Witherspoon St.
Louisville, KY 40202-1396
502/569-5060   FAX 502/569-8090

WORLD COUNCIL OF CHURCHES
150 Route de Ferney
P.O. Box 2100
CH 1211 Geneva 2, Switzerland
                     011-41-22-791-6111
          FAX 011-41-22-798-1346

Topical Index of Hymns and Songs

Ascension
674   Alleluia! Jesus Is Risen!
669   Come Away to the Skies
756   Lord, You Give the Great Commission
Ash Wednesday
732   Create in Me a Clean Heart
659   O Sun of Justice
662   Restore in Us, O God
Assurance   *see Trust/Guidance, Comfort/Rest*
Baptism   *see Holy Baptism*
Baptism of Our Lord, The
647   When Jesus Came to Jordan
Burial   *see Christian Hope, Heaven/Eternal Life*
674   Alleluia! Jesus Is Risen!
699   Blessed Assurance
669   Come Away to the Skies
695   O Blessed Spring
778   O Christ the Same
731   Precious Lord, Take My Hand
741   Thy Holy Wings
675   We Walk by Faith and Not by Sight
Children, Songs for
791   Alabaré
767   All Things Bright and Beautiful
671   Alleluia, Alleluia, Give Thanks
677   Alleluia Canon
644   Away in a Manger
774   Dona Nobis Pacem
788   Glory to God, Glory in the Highest
722   Hallelujah! We Sing Your Praises
660   I Want Jesus to Walk with Me
649   I Want to Walk as a Child of the Light
673   I'm So Glad Jesus Lifted Me
765   Jesu, Jesu, Fill Us with Your Love
740   Jesus, Remember Me
754   Let Us Talents and Tongues Employ
630   Light One Candle to Watch for Messiah
795   Oh, Sing to the Lord
639   Oh, Sleep Now, Holy Baby
643   Once in Royal David's City
690   Shall We Gather at the River
783   Seek Ye First the Kingdom of God
724   Shalom
744   Soon and Very Soon
741   Thy Holy Wings
650   We Are Marching in the Light of God
670   When Israel Was in Egypt's Land
694   You Have Put On Christ
Christ the King/Reign of Christ
740   Jesus, Remember Me
631   Lift Up Your Heads, O Gates
744   Soon and Very Soon
801   Thine the Amen, Thine the Praise
CHRISTIAN HOPE, 742-746
629   All Earth Is Hopeful
674   Alleluia! Jesus Is Risen!
699   Blessed Assurance
736   By Gracious Powers
672   Christ Is Risen! Shout Hosanna!
669   Come Away to the Skies
628   Each Winter As the Year Grows Older
738   Healer of Our Every Ill
777   In the Morning When I Rise
648   Jesus, Come! For We Invite You
695   O Blessed Spring
778   O Christ the Same
762   O Day of Peace
731   Precious Lord, Take My Hand
690   Shall We Gather at the River
691   Sing with All the Saints in Glory
801   Thine the Amen, Thine the Praise
676   This Joyful Eastertide
CHRISTMAS, 636-645
788   Glory to God, Glory in the Highest
634   Sing of Mary, Pure and Lowly
701   What Feast of Love
Church   *see Community in Christ*
Comfort, Rest
       see also Assurance, Trust/Guidance
729   Christ, Mighty Savior

746   Day by Day
738   Healer of Our Every Ill
752   I, the Lord of Sea and Sky
683   Loving Spirit
778   O Christ the Same
731   Precious Lord, Take My Hand
668   There in God's Garden
737   There Is a Balm in Gilead
741   Thy Holy Wings
779   You Who Dwell in the Shelter of the Lord
COMMITMENT, 783-785
652   Arise, Your Light Has Come!
776   Be Thou My Vision
719   God Is Here!
687   Gracious Spirit, Heed Our Pleading
752   I, the Lord of Sea and Sky
713   Lord, Let My Heart Be Good Soil
756   Lord, You Give the Great Commission
684   Spirit, Spirit of Gentleness
755   We All Are One in Mission
Communion of Saints
       see Christian Hope, Heaven/Eternal Life
COMMUNITY IN CHRIST, 747-751
705   As the Grains of Wheat
704   Father, We Thank You
692   For All the Faithful Women
719   God Is Here!
735   God! When Human Bonds Are Broken
708   Grains of Wheat
718   Here in This Place
765   Jesu, Jesu, Fill Us with Your Love
754   Let Us Talents and Tongues Employ
763   Let Justice Flow like Streams
685   Like the Murmur of the Dove's Song
761   Now We Offer
710   One Bread, One Body
724   Shalom
755   We All Are One in Mission
Confession, Forgiveness
       see Forgiveness/Healing
Confirmation
       see Affirmation of Baptism
CREATION, PRESERVATION, 767-771
757   Creating God, Your Fingers Trace
760   For the Fruit of All Creation
794   Many and Great, O God, Are Your Works
726   Oh, Sing to God Above
682   Praise the Spirit in Creation
793   Shout for Joy Loud and Long
684   Spirit, Spirit of Gentleness
799   When Long Before Time
Death   *see Heaven/Eternal Life, Christian Hope, Burial*
Earth   see *Creation/Preservation*
EASTER, 671-679
791   Alabaré
693   Baptized in Water
669   Come Away to the Skies
692   For All the Faithful Women
789   Now the Feast and Celebration
695   O Blessed Spring
793   Shout for Joy Loud and Long
691   Sing with All the Saints in Glory
743   Stay with Us
801   Thine the Amen, Thine the Praise
698   We Were Baptized in Christ Jesus
Easter, Vigil of
693   Baptized in Water
669   Come Away to the Skies
793   Shout for Joy Loud and Long
698   We Were Baptized in Christ Jesus
670   When Israel Was in Egypt's Land
694   You Have Put On Christ
EPIPHANY, 646-654
776   Be Thou My Vision
800   Each Morning Brings Us
638   Holy Child within the Manger
750   Oh, Praise the Gracious Power
755   We All Are One in Mission
716   Word of God, Come Down on Earth
784   You Have Come Down to the Lakeshore

673	I'm So Glad Jesus Lifted Me
781	My Life Flows On in Endless Song
726	Oh, Sing to God Above
795	Oh, Sing to the Lord
793	Shout for Joy Loud and Long

Judgment
629	All Earth Is Hopeful
627	My Lord, What a Morning
744	Soon and Very Soon

Justice   *see Society*

Kingdom of God
764	Blest Are They
718	Here in This Place
740	Jesus, Remember Me
762	O Day of Peace
783	Seek Ye First the Kingdom of God
753	You Are the Seed

Last Times
745	Awake, O Sleeper
627	My Lord, What a Morning
762	O Day of Peace
691	Sing with All the Saints in Glory
744	Soon and Very Soon

LENT, 655-662
745	Awake, O Sleeper
732	Create in Me a Clean Heart
746	Day by Day
738	Healer of Our Every Ill
702	I Am the Bread of Life
739	In All Our Grief
713	Lord, Let My Heart Be Good Soil
769	Mothering God, You Gave Me Birth
695	O Blessed Spring
750	Oh, Praise the Gracious Power
733	Our Father, We Have Wandered
614	Praise to You, O Christ, Our Savior
734	Softly and Tenderly Jesus Is Calling
714	The Thirsty Fields Drink In the Rain
737	There Is a Balm in Gilead
741	Thy Holy Wings
785	Weary of All Trumpeting
716	Word of God, Come Down on Earth
779	You Who Dwell in the Shelter of the Lord

Light
652	Arise, Your Light Has Come!
776	Be Thou My Vision
729	Christ, Mighty Savior
800	Each Morning Brings Us
718	Here in This Place
649	I Want to Walk as a Child of the Light
630	Light One Candle to Watch for Messiah
728	O Light Whose Splendor Thrills
659	O Sun of Justice
651	Shine, Jesus, Shine

Love
664	A New Commandment
751	As Man and Woman We Were Made
666	Great God, Your Love Has Called Us
765	Jesu, Jesu, Fill Us with Your Love
680	O Spirit of Life
665	Ubi Caritas et Amor
749	When Love Is Found
716	Word of God, Come Down on Earth

Marriage
751	As Man and Woman We Were Made
748	Bind Us Together
648	Jesus, Come! For We Invite You
749	When Love Is Found

Maundy Thursday
664	A New Commandment
666	Great God, Your Love Has Called Us
765	Jesu, Jesu, Fill Us with Your Love
667	Stay Here
665	Ubi Caritas et Amor
663	When Twilight Comes

Mary, Mother of Our Lord
692	For All the Faithful Women
730	My Soul Proclaims Your Greatness
634	Sing of Mary, Pure and Lowly
632	The Angel Gabriel from Heaven Came

Ministry
652	Arise, Your Light Has Come!
760	For the Fruit of All Creation
719	God Is Here!
666	Great God, Your Love Has Called Us
752	I, the Lord of Sea and Sky
756	Lord, You Give the Great Commission

Mission   *see Witness*

MORNING, 725-727
633	Awake, Awake, and Greet the New Morn
800	Each Morning Brings Us
771	Great Is Thy Faithfulness
777	In the Morning When I Rise
627	My Lord, What a Morning

Offertory   *see Stewardship*
759	Accept, O Lord, the Gifts We Bring
705	As the Grains of Wheat
758	Come to Us, Creative Spirit
732	Create in Me a Clean Heart
703	Draw Us in the Spirit's Tether
760	For the Fruit of All Creation
708	Grains of Wheat
754	Let Us Talents and Tongues Employ
761	Now We Offer
710	One Bread, One Body
766	We Come to the Hungry Feast

Palm Sunday   *see Sunday of the Passion*

Peace
757	Creating God, Your Fingers Trace
774	Dona Nobis Pacem
763	Let Justice Flow like Streams
781	My Life Flows On in Endless Song
762	O Day of Peace
750	Oh, Praise the Gracious Power
641	Peace Came to Earth
724	Shalom
766	We Come to the Hungry Feast
785	Weary of All Trumpeting
780	What a Fellowship, What a Joy Divine

PENTECOST, THE HOLY SPIRIT, 680-688
719	God Is Here!
775	Lord, Listen to Your Children Praying
756	Lord, You Give the Great Commission

PRAISE, ADORATION, 786-802
782	All My Hope on God Is Founded
671	Alleluia, Alleluia, Give Thanks
674	Alleluia! Jesus Is Risen!
699	Blessed Assurance
747	Christ Is Made the Sure Foundation
717	Come, All You People
758	Come to Us, Creative Spirit
640	Gloria *(Taizé)*
637	Gloria, Gloria, Gloria
719	God Is Here!
722	Hallelujah! We Sing Your Praises
720	In the Presence of Your People
631	Lift Up Your Heads, O Gates
730	My Soul Proclaims Your Greatness
726	Oh, Sing to God Above
635	Surely It Is God Who Saves Me

PRAYER, 772-775
740	Jesus, Remember Me
783	Seek Ye First the Kingdom of God
667	Stay Here

Reconciliation   *see Forgiveness/Healing*
745	Awake, O Sleeper
735	God! When Human Bonds Are Broken
738	Healer of Our Every Ill
762	O Day of Peace
750	Oh, Praise the Gracious Power

Reformation Day
747	Christ Is Made the Sure Foundation
756	Lord, You Give the Great Commission
750	Oh, Praise the Gracious Power
755	We All Are One in Mission

Repentance   *see Forgiveness/Healing*

Saints' Days
692	For All the Faithful Women
689	Rejoice in God's Saints
691	Sing with All the Saints in Glory

Scriptural Index of Hymns and Songs

Text and Music Sources

Tunes—Alphabetical

Tunes—Metrical

8 8 4 4 6 and refrain
THREE KINGS OF ORIENT 646
8 8 and refrain
ALLELUIA NO.1 671
8 8 4 9
CONVIVIO 714
8 8 7 4 and refrain
HIS NAME SO SWEET 696
8 8 8 8 8 8
RYBURN 666
SUSSEX CAROL 751
8 8 8 8 8 8 8 6
MARVEL 636
8 8 9 and refrain
HEALER OF OUR EVERY ILL 738
8 8 9 9 9 7 7 7
DAPIT HAPON 663
8 10 10 and refrain
PESCADOR DE HOMBRES 784
9 6 8 8 8 6
LAC QUI PARLE 794
9 6 9 6 6
CAROL OF HOPE 628
9 7 9 6 D
WATERLIFE 770
9 8 9 5 and refrain
YISRAEL V'ORAITA 715
9 8 9 8
ST. CLEMENT 728
9 8 9 8 D
RENDEZ À DIEU 704
9 8 9 8 8 7 8 9
REJOICE, REJOICE 633
9 9 9 9 and refrain
MFURAHINI, HALELUYA 678
9 9 10 10 3 3 and refrain
SHINE, JESUS, SHINE 651
9 10 9 9 and refrain
ASSURANCE 699
10 7 9 6
TIF IN VELDELE 630
10 7 10 8 and refrain
HOUSTON 649
10 8 8 8 10
O HEILIGER GEIST 680
O JESULEIN SÜSS 680
10 9 10 8 D and refrain
ID Y ENSEÑAD 753
10 9 10 9 and refrain
SHOWALTER 780
10 9 10 9 D
BLOTT EN DAG 746
10 9 10 10 D
GATHER US IN 718
10 10 9 10
SLANE 776
10 10 10 and refrain
FREDERICKTOWN 739
10 10 10 4
ENGELBERG 802
10 10 10 8 8
SCHNEIDER 641
10 10 10 10
WOODLANDS 787
10 10 11 11
LAUDATE DOMINUM 689
10 10 12 10
GABRIEL'S MESSAGE 632
10 10 13 10
UNA ESPIGA 708
11 7 11 7 and refrain
THOMPSON 734

11 10 11 10
BERLIN 736
11 10 11 10 and refrain
FAITHFULNESS 771
11 10 11 10 D
LONDONDERRY AIR 778
11 11 11 5
INNISFREE FARM 729
SHADES MOUNTAIN 668
11 11 11 11
CRADLE SONG 644
THE SINGER AND THE SONG 799
11 11 12 12
TAULÉ 629
12 11 11 12
I WONDER 642
12 12 12 and refrain
VERY SOON 744
13 13 13 13 13 13
THAXTED 797
14 14 15 14
THINE 801
irregular
A LA RU 639
ALABARÉ 791
AMEN SIAKUDUMISA 786
AMIN HALELUYA 792
AS THE GRAINS 705
BALM IN GILEAD 737
BAPTIZED IN CHRIST 694
BERTHIER 709
BLEST ARE THEY 764
BREAD OF LIFE 702
CAUSE OF OUR JOY 707
CHILDREN PRAYING 775
DONA NOBIS PACEM 774
FRANCKE 732
GLORIA 3 640
GLORIA CUECA 637
GLORIA PERU 788
GOOD SOIL 713
HALELUYA! PELO TSO RONA 722
I AM THE BREAD 702
JESUS LIFTED ME 673
LAFFERTY 783
MOZART ALLELUIA 677
NEW COMMANDMENT 664
NOW THE FEAST 789
ON EAGLE'S WINGS 779
PRAISE PSALM 103 798
PRECIOUS LORD 731
REMEMBER ME 740
RISE UP, SHEPHERD 645
SHALOM 724
SIYAHAMBA 650
SOJOURNER 660
SPIRIT 684
STAY HERE 667
TAIZÉ UBI CARITAS 665
TAIZÉ VENI SANCTE 686
THANKS BE TO YOU 790
THE CELEBRATION SONG 720
THUMA MINA 773
WA EMIMIMO 681

First Lines and Common Titles

ISBN 0-8066-0051-9

9 780806 600512 90000